PLATO
PHAEDRUS

PLATO
PHAEDRUS

Translated,
with Introduction
and Notes, by

ALEXANDER NEHAMAS

&

PAUL WOODRUFF

with a selection of early Greek
poems and fragments about love, translated
by Paul Woodruff

Hackett Publishing Company, Inc.
Indianapolis/Cambridge

Plato: ca. 428–347 B.C.

Copyright © 1995 by Alexander Nehamas & Paul Woodruff
All rights reserved
Printed in the United States of America

4 5 6 7 8 9 10 11 12
10 09 08 07 06 05

For further information, please
address the publisher:

Hackett Publishing Company
P.O. Box 44937
Indianapolis, Indiana 46244-0937

Cover illustration:
Horse of Selene,
from the East Pediment of the Parthenon,
ca. 438–431 B.C.
London, British Museum

Interior design by Dan Kirklin

Library of Congress Cataloging-in-Publication Data

Plato
[Phaedrus. English]
Phaedrus/translated, with introduction & notes, by
Alexander Nehamas & Paul Woodruff.
p. cm.
Includes bibliographical references (p.   ).
ISBN 0-87220-221-6   ISBN 0-87220-220-8 pbk.
1. Rhetoric, Ancient—Early works to 1800.
2. Love—Early works to 1800.
3. Soul—Early works to 1800.
4. Socrates—Early works to 1800.
5. Lysias—Early works to 1800.
I. Nehamas, Alexander, 1946–
II. Woodruff, Paul, 1943–
III. Title.
B380.A5N44 1995
184—dc20   94-46613
CIP

CONTENTS

Preface　　vii
Introduction　　ix
Outline of the *Phaedrus*　　xlix

Phaedrus　　1

Appendix: Early Greek Love Poetry　　87
Selected Bibliography　　93

PREFACE

This work, like our translation of the *Symposium*, is a joint product. Paul Woodruff prepared the first draft of the speeches in the *Phaedrus* and wrote the notes to the translation; Alexander Nehamas produced the first draft of the conversation between Socrates and Phaedrus and wrote the introduction. We then went over all of each other's work as carefully as we could, on a number of occasions. We wish to thank John Cooper, whose comments on every aspect of this book have improved, again, virtually every page. Paul Woodruff also acknowledges the help of Anne Farrell and Mark Gifford with the speeches, and of Harvey Hix and Stanley Lombardo with his translations of Greek poetry in the Appendix.

Full bibliographical information on works referred to only in the Introduction will be found in the footnotes. The Selected Bibliography lists all the works referred to in the notes to the translation as well as other works relevant to the *Phaedrus*. In the notes, we refer to the commentaries by de Vries, Hackforth, and Rowe by their authors' names.

INTRODUCTION

General Remarks

ODYSSEUS HAD NEVER WANTED to take part in the Greek expedition against Troy that is the subject of Homer's *Iliad*: strange and dangerous things often happen away from home. He pretended to be mad, but the great trickster was himself tricked by Palamedes into admitting his sanity and joining the departing armies.[1] Odysseus, however, may have been right not to want to leave Ithaca. None of the Greek heroes met with so many troubles and strange adventures, and none was absent as long as Odysseus, who spent twenty years abroad before finally returning home.

In the *Phaedrus*, Plato strikes an unusual variation on the theme of leaving home—of abandoning, even for a short while, the surroundings to which one is accustomed. We know from another of his dialogues, the *Crito*, that Socrates never left Athens for any reason except military service; he even refused to attend festivals that were held in the countryside, and he had no desire to know what life in other cities was like (*Crito* 52d). Phaedrus himself remarks here that Socrates is totally out of place (*atopōtatos*) in the country: "Not only do you never travel abroad," he says; "as far as I can tell, you never even set foot beyond the city walls" (230d).

But Socrates *has* set foot beyond the city walls on this occasion. The *Phaedrus* is the only Platonic dialogue in which Socrates

---

1. To prove that he was mad, Odysseus took to plowing a rocky piece of land where nothing could grow. Palamedes, however, placed Odysseus' infant son, Telemachus, on the plow's path. Odysseus then swerved in order not to kill the child, and his madness was shown to have been a ruse. This story is not mentioned either in the *Iliad* or in the *Odyssey*, but it can be found in Hyginus' *Fabulae* or *Genealogiae*, 277.1.

leaves the city in order to engage in philosophical conversation.[2] And even though he only takes a short walk in the country, what happens to him is in a way stranger than any of Odysseus' adventures. Odysseus, after all, survived the dangers and monsters he faced by staying the same, by acting as he always had before: with craftiness, wiliness, courage, and prudence. But Socrates seems to become almost a different person once he leaves Athens. Odysseus met external enemies: strange gods, weird monsters, unknown peoples. Socrates, who claims that, not "knowing himself," he wonders whether he is "a beast more complicated and savage than Typho, or . . . a tamer, simpler animal with a share in a divine and gentle nature,"[3] discovers by the banks of the river Ilisus parts of himself he had never known before. The "monsters" he meets, though not malevolent, come from within.

Why, then, does he leave? Because Phaedrus, cast here in a role a bit like that of Palamedes, tricks him into abandoning his usual urban haunts.[4] More accurately, Phaedrus lures him outside the city with the promise that he will read to him a speech on love (*erōs*) which Lysias, the great orator of the final years of the fifth century B.C., had just composed. Socrates, who confesses that he is "sick with passion for hearing speeches" and calls himself "a lover of speeches" (228b–c), tells Phaedrus that he would follow him to the ends of the earth in order to hear what Lysias has to say on the topic (227d). And so the two friends look for a place in the country where they can listen to the speech in comfort and quiet.

Odysseus pretended to be mad in order to stay home and survived abroad by the powers of his reason. Socrates, who is the

---

2. It should be noted that the *Republic* describes a conversation that takes place in the Piraeus, Athens' port. But the two localities were adjacent, connected by the famous "Long Walls" which were destroyed when Athens lost the Peloponnesian War in 404 B.C. In a literal sense, going to Piraeus (which Socrates may well have done more than once) was not going beyond the city walls.

3. See 230a and nn. 14 and 15 to the translation.

4. Palamedes appears, in a different context, in the *Phaedrus*. See 261b and n. 139.

Introduction

embodiment of reason in Athens, seems to lose his composure, if not his mind, the moment he leaves the city. His uncharacteristically lyrical praise of the spot where they have chosen to sit stuns Phaedrus. Socrates replies that the promise of hearing the speech has worked magic on him; like a donkey marching endlessly in fruitless pursuit of feed dangled in front of its nose, he will follow Phaedrus wherever he goes as long as he is carrying Lysias' speech (229b–230e).[5]

The very idea that the prospect of listening to a speech would have such an effect on Socrates is surprising; it should alert us to the exceptional nature of the situation portrayed in this dialogue. Socrates, as Plato pictures him, has never been "a lover of speeches." On the contrary, he has consistently expressed his aversion to long discourses. Throughout the dialogues, he insists that he can only discuss matters by means of the short question-and-answer method we know as the elenchus: he can neither make nor indeed understand long speeches (see, e.g., *Protagoras* 334c–335c, *Gorgias* 449b–c, 461d–462a). In the *Phaedrus*, however, he not only listens avidly to Lysias' speech; he also criticizes it and even produces two long speeches of his own, one of which, the second or "Great Speech" (243e–257b), is one of the most famous rhetorical accomplishments of classical Greece.

What has happened to change Socrates so radically? His own explanation is that he has come to be possessed by the gods and spirits that inhabit the enchanted place where he and Phaedrus have found themselves: the speeches he makes, he insists again and again, are not his own creations but theirs (235c–d, 238d, 241e–242a, 262c–d). Of course Socrates in the *Phaedrus* and these other works is Plato's own creation. And the question we need to ask is not primarily why Socrates is behaving so strangely in

---

5. This simile is only one aspect of the *Phaedrus* that anticipates some of the strange happenings in Shakespeare's *Midsummer Night's Dream*: Socrates is not the only literary character to have been enchanted by the woods surrounding ancient Athens. In Shakespeare's play, Bottom is given a donkey's head by Puck; and Titania, the queen of the fairies, is made to fall in love with him. Four lovers—Lysander, Demetrius, Helena, and Hermia—also find their affections strangely changed once they have left Athens for the countryside.

this case, but rather why Plato has taken his very urban and rational Socrates and made him willing to leave Athens, vulnerable to possession by the nymphs (*numpholēptos*, 238d) and by the gods (*enthousiazōn*, 241e) and capable of composing such magnificent orations. For, in the process, Plato has himself produced one of the strangest dialogues he ever wrote. The whole of the *Phaedrus*, no less than Socrates or the magical place where its action takes place, is an unending source of enchantment, of unexpected situations, of puzzlement and speculation.

Though the *Phaedrus* is one of Plato's greatest and most widely read dialogues, its structure constitutes a perennial subject of debate. Since later antiquity, its central subject has commonly been taken to be the way in which love leads to philosophy—the subject of Socrates' second speech. After all, Plato had already addressed that very idea in the *Symposium*, another work consisting almost entirely of speeches; and the *Phaedrus*, with its three speeches on love, is commonly taken as its companion piece. Our interest in the *Phaedrus* often centers on the question of how the metaphysics, epistemology, and psychology of the *Republic*, which was written after the *Symposium* and in all probability before the *Phaedrus*, affect the view of *erōs* presented in the latter work.[6] And the magnificence of Socrates' Great Speech, which is a panegyric on love and quite overwhelms the rest of the work, makes it difficult to believe that anything other than *erōs* could be Plato's central topic. But if the speeches contain Plato's main topic, why does the long discussion of rhetoric that follows them never address their substance? If love is the main theme of the *Phaedrus*, why is it forgotten in the dialogue's second half?

In order to be able to address the question of the structure of the *Phaedrus* as a whole, we must first make some remarks about the nature of its parts.

****

---

6. An interesting argument to the effect that Plato does not have, in any strict sense, a theory of *erōs* is offered by G.R.F. Ferrari, "Platonic Love." It should also be said that there is no firm external evidence that the *Phaedrus* was in fact written after the *Republic*. However, the

INTRODUCTION

The *Phaedrus* is an account of a conversation between Socrates and Phaedrus. It is impossible to pinpoint the "dramatic date" of the work, that is, the time when that conversation is supposed to have taken place. In fact, there doesn't seem to have been a time when this meeting between Phaedrus and Socrates could have occurred. Because of his alleged involvement in the notorious mutilation of the statues of the god Hermes, Phaedrus was exiled from Athens from 415, when the crime was committed, until 403 B.C. The conversation cannot have occurred between 403 and 399 B.C., when Socrates was executed, since there is a strong indication that Sophocles and Euripides, who both died in 406 B.C., are still alive when the action of the dialogue takes place (268c). It is also unlikely to have occurred any earlier than 415, before Phaedrus' exile, because Lysias, whose company Phaedrus has just left as the dialogue opens, lived abroad in the city of Thurii in Italy for a number of years and returned to Athens only in 412, after Phaedrus had already left.

We can be a little more positive about the *Phaedrus*' date of composition: that is, the time when Plato actually wrote the dialogue. It seems to be later than the *Republic*, close to the *Parmenides*, and earlier than the *Sophist*.[7] Although, like most efforts to date Plato's works, this view partly depends on speculation, we can say with some confidence that the *Phaedrus* was written between 375 and 365 B.C., at the time when Plato was

---

most coherent account of Plato's philosophical development depends on the relative dating of the works assumed here, and defended below.

7. Socrates' second speech seems to allude to many of the ideas Plato expressed in the *Meno*, the *Phaedo*, and the *Republic*. They include the view that knowledge is recollection, the idea of the transmigration of the soul, and the assumption that the Forms are perfect exemplars of the qualities for which they stand: thus, for example, the Form of Beauty is the most beautiful thing in existence. The brief discussion of collection and division (265c–266c) as the correct method of pursuing philosophical issues anticipates its detailed application in the *Sophist*. If we assume that the *Parmenides*, in which the theory of Forms of the *Republic* comes under criticism, was written between the *Republic* and the *Sophist*, in which a new method of dialectic is followed, then it is reasonable to suppose that the *Phaedrus* was written not long before or after that work.

entering the third phase of his philosophical development, following his early, Socratic period and his middle phase, which is associated with the flourishing of the theory of Forms as most people know it today.

****

The *Phaedrus* is a dialogue in the most literal sense. Unlike a number of others of Plato's works, it is a conversation between two and only two people.[8] Phaedrus, who is a mature man when this conversation is supposed to have taken place,[9] is portrayed as a great admirer of Lysias in particular and of rhetoric in general. Though a friend of Socrates, he seems to have little appreciation or understanding of Socrates' approach to life and thought. He loves rhetoric, but he seems to think of it as a contest aiming to produce a more novel or comprehensive speech than one's opponent that ends only when one of the contestants is forced to give up (see 243d, 257c). His attitude toward philosophy is not unlike his approach to rhetoric. Though he thinks that life

---

8. Other dialogues that fall in this category include the *Euthyphro*, the *Crito*, the *Ion*, the *Hippias Major*, the *Hippias Minor*, and the *Menexenus*.

9. At 236b, Socrates refers to Lysias as Phaedrus' *paidika*, that is, as the boy with whom Phaedrus, in the position of an older man, is in love. The point may be a joke, but it strongly suggests that Phaedrus cannot be younger than Lysias. Similarly, at 257b, Socrates says that Phaedrus is Lysias' *erastēs*, thus reinforcing the same point. At 242a–b he claims that Phaedrus has himself produced or caused others to produce more speeches than any of his contemporaries, with the exception of Simmias of Thebes; this too suggests that he cannot be a very young man at the time of this discussion. There is no evidence in the dialogue to suggest that Phaedrus is himself a young boy trying to decide what sort of life—and lover—he should choose or that the work revolves centrally around that issue (as argued by Nussbaum, *The Fragility of Goodness*, ch. 7). Though Socrates does occasionally address Phaedrus as *pai* (roughly, "child") and *neania* (roughly, "youth," "young man"), this is not telling. Such terms of intimacy were as common then as they are now. Consider, for example, that Socrates refers to Agathon, who is thirty years old, as a *meirakion* (roughly, "adolescent boy") at *Symposium* 223a.

would be unbearable without the pleasures of philosophical conversation (258e), it is not clear that he understands the profound effect that philosophical ideas can have on one's life. Socrates' Great Speech may in fact be intended to convince him, as far as a man of his character can be convinced on that issue, that philosophy is life's most serious activity.

Socrates describes Phaedrus as a "begetter" of speeches (261a). His description is justified by Phaedrus' eagerness to memorize Lysias' speech, by his insistence that Socrates compete with Lysias with speeches of his own, and by the fact that the idea of praising *erōs* in the *Symposium*, where Phaedrus is characterized as "the father of the subject," was originally his own. But Phaedrus' seriousness does not match his enthusiasm. Socrates makes a great effort to get Phaedrus to realize that rhetoric must be pursued with a regard for the truth of what one is talking about. And since truth is what we get to know through philosophy, Socrates argues that philosophy is a necessary element in the rhetorician's art. In addition, Socrates wants him to understand that rhetoric and philosophy, whether in oral or written form, are not simply means of urbane entertainment but efforts to establish views according to which life can be led. Whether Phaedrus learns either lesson in the course of his conversation with Socrates remains an open question at the end of the dialogue.

PART ONE: INTRODUCTION AND SPEECHES (227a–257b)

The *Phaedrus* falls naturally into two parts. The first (227a–257b) consists of an introductory conversation and three speeches on *erōs*.

The kind of love addressed by the three speeches is almost exclusively love between men—a central feature in the life of the ancient Greeks in general and the Athenians in particular.[10] Today, such relationships are often called "homosexual,"[11] but

---

10. For a general discussion of the subject, see Dover, *Greek Homosexuality*; and Foucault, *The Uses of Pleasure*.
11. We ourselves followed that usage in our introduction to our translation of Plato's *Symposium*.

the term should be used with care. "Homosexuality" usually denotes an exclusive sexual preference for members of one's own sex and, often, a particular style of life that revolves around it. In ancient Athens, however, though there were men who lived exclusively with other men, as we learn, for example, in regard to Pausanias and Agathon in the *Symposium* (193b–c),[12] most paederastic relationships were different from what we now consider homosexual affairs.

It was a common though by no means a universally approved practice in ancient Athens for older men to fall in love with young, usually adolescent, boys. Such a difference in age, which may or may not form part of homosexual relationships, was essential to paederasty. In addition, paederasty did not in general interfere with marriage or other relationships with women. The older man (*erastēs*) would most often already be married, while the younger one (*erōmenos*) would be expected to marry when he reached the appropriate age.

In paederastic affairs, the boy was expected not to give in easily to his admirer, who was in turn expected to engage in passionate and extravagant gestures of love and devotion. Even if the boy was finally won over, it was not expected that the sexual encounter would bring him great pleasure—at least it was expected that he would not show signs of being pleased too readily. What was expected was that the *erastēs* would act as an ethical and intellectual teacher of his *erōmenos*. What the two participants thus took from their relationship was, at least in theory, radically different: the older man received pleasure; the younger, education and edification. Paederasty was in many cases an instrument of socialization and teaching.

In his speech (230d–234c), Lysias focuses on this aspect of paederastic relationships and turns it around to his own paradoxical purposes.[13] The speaker urges a young boy to accept him as a lover precisely because the older man is not in love with him, and argues that in general someone who does not love a boy will be better for him, as a friend and teacher, than someone

---

12. Aristophanes actually parodied Agathon's effeminate ways in his *Thesmophoriazousai*.
13. On the authorship of this speech, see note 19 to the translation.

INTRODUCTION xvii

who does. The central idea of the speech is that love makes men passionate while it lasts, but, once it is gone, makes them at best indifferent to, at worst enemies of, their earlier loves. By contrast, a man who enters into a sexual relationship with a boy without love does so "with no thought of immediate pleasure; [he] will plan instead for the benefits that are to come, since [he] is master of [himself] and [has] not been overwhelmed by love" (233b–c). Non-lovers, the speaker argues, are much more likely to become and remain friends (*philoi*). The whole speech depends on an exaggerated interpretation of the utilitarian aspects of paederasty: the basic premise is that if education and long-lasting friendship are the goals of such relationships, non-lovers are much more likely to secure them for boys than are lovers. The speaker paradoxically appears to renounce *erōs* (which involves passionate sexual desire) as a ploy to gain sexual favors.

Lysias' speech, which turns all accepted ideas about paederasty on their head, is what is known as an "epideictic" speech. Epideictic speeches were exhibition works. They were intended to show what a speech writer was capable of doing even with an unpromising subject. They often functioned as advertisements for their authors' talents. The more unusual the position supported, and the better argued it was, the better the advertisement. Phaedrus clearly thinks of Lysias' speech as an immense accomplishment, and is eager to have Socrates agree with his view.

****

Socrates, though, will have none of it. He claims that the speech is both crudely constructed and repetitive. The fact that he is willing to criticize the speech at all, instead of pleading, as usual, ignorance of rhetoric, is already surprising enough. But this is only the first of many surprising events in this work. The next is about to occur.

Socrates has already indicated that he finds himself in an unusually inspired state (234d). He now claims that he has heard much better speeches on the same topic. He is not sure whether they are the work of Sappho or Anacreon (the great early love poets of ancient Greece) or of some other author. But he is sure of the following: "My breast is full," he tells Phaedrus, "and I feel I can make a different speech, even better than Lysias'. Now I am well aware that none of these ideas can have come from me—I know my own ignorance. The only other possibility, I think, is that I was filled, like an empty jar, by the words of other people streaming in through my ears" (235c–d). Though he does not completely deny his ignorance, Socrates claims, for once in all of Plato's work, to be able to deliver a speech.[14]

So an inspired Socrates, though unwilling to accept full responsibility for what he is about to say, proceeds to make his own speech on Lysias' subject (237b–241d). He begins with a definition of love as an irrational impulse that overpowers our desire to do what is right and attracts us inescapably to beauty. On the basis of this definition and a stark contrast between reason, which desires the good, and irrational impulse, which seeks pleasure and gratification, he argues that the lover is bound to be harmful to the boys he pursues. *Erōs* is a kind of madness, and all madness—especially the madness of love—must be avoided at all costs: it will destroy the soul as well as the body of the boy; it will consume his property, provoke his disgust, and ultimately leave him without a friend and protector. Socrates' speech is a direct counterpart to Lysias'; all that Socrates leaves out is the complementary argument that the non-lover is beneficial. His speech, that is, stops short before the explicit attempt at seduction.

In this way, Socrates produces a counter-epideictic speech and makes an implicit claim to have beaten the orator at his own game. This, naturally, is a very peculiar situation, since Lysias is one of the great orators of the time, while Socrates officially disavows any knowledge of rhetoric. We must therefore keep in mind the question of what it is that Plato is trying to suggest by having Socrates outdo Lysias even though Socrates claims to have no knowledge of rhetoric as such knowledge was understood at the time.

---

14. Socrates, of course, also delivers a speech on *erōs* in the *Symposium*. But there he explicitly attributes the speech to Diotima, and even delivers it as if it were coming directly from her. There is no explicit acknowledgment within the fictional world of the *Symposium* (though Plato gives a number of hints to that effect to his readers) as there is in the *Phaedrus* that the speech is really his own.

INTRODUCTION

But Socrates' victory is hollow. Deeply dissatisfied with his performance, he claims that his "divine sign" (see *Apology* 31c–d) has let him know that he should not leave the place where he and Phaedrus have found themselves before he makes amends for a very grave error on his part. What is that error? It is the very speech he has just given—even though he had earlier claimed that the speech was not his own but something he had heard from others, perhaps even the product of divine inspiration. Socrates, that is, acknowledges that he is far from completely free of responsibility for what is wrong with his speech. And what is wrong with the speech is that it attacks *erōs* because, being a kind of madness, it is worse than and cannot be preferred to any rational state of mind. Socrates' first speech, therefore, is an argument to the effect that *erōs* is an evil to be avoided—an argument which represents a conventional (if playful) stance in early Greek love poetry.[15]

****

Socrates, however, is now faced with the feeling that his first speech was blasphemous, since *erōs* is a god or at least something divine (242e) and cannot therefore be bad in any of the ways his speech had asserted.[16] In an exchange full of religious and mythological allusions, he recants his earlier speech and claims that he cannot absolve himself unless he makes another speech, this time in praise of *erōs* (241d–243e).

Socrates' second speech is for many of Plato's readers the

---

15. An Appendix consisting of a sample of early Greek love poetry follows the translation of the *Phaedrus*.
16. Some commentators, e.g., Rowe (p. 166), find serious differences between the view of *erōs* expressed here and the discussion in the *Symposium* (201e–203b), where *erōs* is said to be not a god but a spirit, and neither good nor bad, but "in between" the two. But we should not exaggerate these differences. Plato's present statement that *erōs* is "a god or something divine" is compatible with *erōs* being a "spirit" (*daimōn*); and his view that he therefore "can't be bad in any way" is compatible with his not being good—which are just the positions he had taken in the *Symposium*.

centerpiece of the *Phaedrus*.[17] The speech is a magnificent, imaginative construction; it leaves the two that precede it so far behind that it is sometimes difficult even to remember that they actually form part of the dialogue. The first two speeches recount the disadvantages of *erōs* when it comes to capturing the affections of a boy. The Great Speech is a hymn to the indispensability of *erōs* for human life as a whole. The other speeches consist of playful arguments seeking love while denying it; they are firmly located within the world of everyday life. The third speech constructs, by means of argument and myth, a grandiose and apparently serious picture of the human soul and its fate, both when it is embodied and when, free of the body, it travels across the heavens in the company of the Olympian gods. *Erōs*, as Socrates had argued in his earlier speech, still turns out to be a kind of madness, but madness is no longer assumed to be necessarily bad. On the contrary, Socrates now credits it with some of the greatest gifts with which human life is blessed. *Erōs* emerges as the moving force behind the best possible human life. And as we might well expect when Plato addresses the question of the best human life, that life turns out to be the life of the philosophers. As in the *Symposium*, *erōs* leads to philosophy. But in contrast to the *Symposium*, where its irrational aspects receive little if any notice, in the *Phaedrus* *erōs* is primarily a madness—a madness, moreover, that enables us to live in a truly rational manner. The paradoxical conclusions of the earlier speeches are swept aside by the far greater paradox presented in this praise of love: Losing one's mind is a prerequisite for truly finding it and for living according to the values reason dictates. But the speech, as we shall eventually see, is not without its own playful side; Socrates, in fact, describes it by that term himself at 268c.

Socrates begins his speech with the claim that madness, which he had classified as an evil in his first speech, is much more complex than he had allowed there. Many benefits, he argues, come to us through madness; he mentions the importance of the madness of prophets and seers, the madness that sometimes

---

17. On this tendency (which he traces back to Marcilio Ficino), see Christopher Rowe, "The Argument and Structure of Plato's *Phaedrus*," pp. 105–107 with notes.

Introduction

presages absolution from family curses, and the madness of poets (244a–245b). He then leaves this topic and turns to a proof of the immortality of the human soul; the soul, he argues, is a self-moving thing and the principle of motion for everything else. But the principle of motion must be ever-moving: if it ever stopped, everything else would also come to a stop; and if the soul were to start moving again, it would have to do so by means of some further principle—which would show that it was not a principle after all. And since life and motion go hand in hand, the soul, ever-moving as it is, is also ever-living (245b–246a).

At this point, Socrates abandons the logical style he has used in his proof of the soul's immortality and produces what he explicitly describes as a simile (cf. *eoiketō*, 246a) for its structure. He likens the soul to a winged two-horse chariot driven by a charioteer. The teams that correspond to the souls of the gods (or perhaps to the gods themselves) are in perfect internal harmony.[18] But in all other cases the charioteer has an uneasy relationship with his horses. One of them is docile and obedient, while the other is wild and (so to speak) has a mind of its own. The winged soul lives by itself, independently of body. But when souls lose their wings, they fall downward from heaven and enter bodies, to which they impart motion and life: such complexes of body and soul constitute what we call mortal animals (246a–d).

The chariots of the gods, each followed by the souls that are the god's natural companions, travel around heaven and regularly see from its outer rim a "place beyond" which it is impossible to describe accurately: "What is in this place is without color and without shape and without solidity, a being that really is what it is, the subject of all true knowledge, visible only to intelligence, the soul's steersman" (247c). Reason, which is what

---

18. Whether Plato's simile envisages that the gods have souls or that they simply are souls is not absolutely clear. Many points in Socrates' second speech are obscure in this way. Consider, for example, the rather obscure description of "the place beyond heaven" a little further on (246c–247d), or the issue of the extent of the soul's wings: do they belong to the horses only (246a) or to the whole complex (251b–c)? The speech leaves many such questions open, and we should not be too insistent in pressing it for answers.

the charioteer stands for in Plato's simile, is nourished by this otherwise invisible being, which includes true justice, true self-control, true knowledge, and all the other objects which in his middle dialogues Plato had called the Forms and which constitute the world's real and ultimate structure.

But while the gods circle the outer rim of the heavens without trouble, the crowds of the lesser souls that follow them are fighting with one another for a glimpse of the place beyond heaven's rim and of the beings that would nourish them. Their view is therefore partial. Some, indeed, succeed in seeing enough to remain aloft. Many, undernourished as they are, have their wings broken as they jostle one another in their effort to rise above heaven. Without wings, they fall earthward, enter human bodies, and lead different lives, in accordance with how much contact they had with the Forms while they were still disembodied. Those who had the best view become philosophers, lovers of beauty, cultivated people, or devotees of erotic love. Those who saw the least become tyrants—rulers of cities who, according to the eighth and ninth books of the *Republic*, are the most contemptible human beings because they are slaves to desires which are in fact impossible to satisfy.

There thus begins a cycle of reincarnation that lasts for ten thousand years—it takes that long, Socrates says, for the soul to grow its wings again. The only exception is provided by those souls that choose the life of a philosopher or of the right sort of lover of boys who combines *erōs* with philosophy: these souls can return to the heavens after three reincarnations and within three thousand years. The others keep choosing new lives every thousand years, sometimes going from human to beast, sometimes the other way around. The most important factor in this cycle is how much the disembodied soul had seen of the Forms while it was traveling around heaven. The more one has seen, the more truly human one is. For to be truly human is to think abstractly, and abstract thought is nothing but "the recollection of the things a soul saw when it was traveling with gods, when it disregarded the things we now call real and lifted up its head to what is truly real instead" (249b). Such recollection, which Plato had discussed in the *Meno* and in the *Phaedo*, is precisely the activity of philosophers. Philosophers have little regard for merely human affairs; they live, so to speak, in another world;

everyone else therefore thinks that they are mad instead of realizing that they are the most sane and perfect of human beings (246d–249d).

The reference to the apparent madness of philosophers brings Socrates back to his original account of the benefits of madness in general. He now introduces a fourth kind of madness—the kind "which someone shows when he sees the beauty we have down here and is reminded of true beauty," the Form of Beauty in the place beyond heaven. This is the madness of love (249d). Recollection, he says, is very hard: our souls have seen little of the Forms, whose images on the earth are very indistinct. But there is one glorious exception—Beauty. Beauty "was radiant" when our souls traveled the heavens; and, unlike the other Forms, its earthly images enter our soul through vision, the sharpest of our senses, and are therefore much stronger than those of the rest. What counts as an image of Beauty? Socrates' answer is clear: In the best case, it is a beautiful boy who is no longer an object of value simply in himself but also as a reminder of the true Beauty which nourishes our soul and provides, eventually, a way out of the circle of reincarnation.

Those people who retain enough of their memory of Beauty are so taken with the boy's beauty that they are ready to worship him as a god. Their souls' wings begin to grow again. Plato uses a protracted metaphor, describing sexual excitement and the general agitation that overtakes a man in love in terms of the soul's feathers growing, swelling, and piercing their covering. The man literally loses his mind. He is willing to do anything for the boy he loves, to give up everything, to follow him wherever he goes, and to sleep at his doorstep—even if it is merely to catch a fleeting glimpse of him.

Erōs, then, is losing one's mind to Beauty. It is superficially directed at the boy, but the ultimate driving force behind it is the recollection of and the desire to possess again the Beauty which the soul saw during its disembodied travels. Moreover, Beauty itself is a proxy for the rest of the Forms, which it helps us recollect, however imperfectly, and which it makes us desire all the more. The earthly images of Beauty, the beautiful boys who were treated in such a cavalier fashion in the previous two speeches, now turn out to be our closest link to immortality and to a life that, by devoting itself to the recollection of the Forms, is our best road back to that blessed state: the stakes have been radically raised (249d–253c).

But *erōs* is not easy. Falling in love with a boy does not by itself guarantee that one will become a philosopher. The complexity of the soul, which is represented in Plato's simile by the charioteer and his two horses and recalls in many details the tripartition of the soul in the fourth book of the *Republic* (and its further elaboration in books eight and nine), explains why people react so differently to sexual and erotic desire. The charioteer (reason) and the obedient horse (the "spirited" element of the *Republic*, whose goal is honor) work together; but the second horse, which represents the appetitive part, works against them. While the first two hold themselves back from treating the boy improperly, the wild horse keeps pulling the whole soul forward and close to the boy so that it can accomplish its own goal—sexual pleasure.

Socrates describes the conflict in the soul in detailed and moving terms. In the process, Plato offers a highly revisionary account of paederasty. According to this account, sexual gratification is the goal neither of the boy nor, much more surprisingly, of the *erastēs*. Plato admits that most often, of course, the lover gives in to the wild horse and uses the boy only for his pleasure. But in a few cases, after a long and painful struggle, the wild horse is subdued. The lover now respects the boy and approaches him only in the proper manner, as a good friend. The boy gradually begins to be attracted by the older man and his obvious good will; and as they spend more and more time together, he in turn begins to fall in love with the man. But his love, Socrates points out, is not really love for the man himself, who, after all, does not even have to be beautiful. Rather, it is (though the boy does not know this) love for his own image reflected back at him through his lover's eyes: he too, then, begins to fall in love with the image of Beauty he himself constitutes and therefore, indirectly, with Beauty itself.

Even companionship of the best sort, however, brings the two lovers in close physical contact, and the wild horse once again asserts its need and desire. Socrates describes two outcomes. The lovers may overpower their appetite completely and spend their time together chastely devoted to philosophy—that is, to the effort to recollect and understand the nature of true Beauty, Justice, Virtue, and the other Forms. If this is how they live, he claims, they will die happy and have to face only two more reincarnations of the same sort before their souls are liberated from their bonds to mortal body and return to heaven. But some lovers may be weaker than the previous pair. They may give in to their sexual urges and consummate their love affair in a way that, for Plato, is far from ideal. But it needn't be too far: provided that sex is not the main goal of their relationship and that they treat each other properly in a serious and long-lasting friendship, there is a good chance that, upon their death, they will begin a longer but ultimately successful voyage back to the disembodied state which, Socrates argues here, constitutes human perfection (253c–256e).

The central idea of Lysias' speech was that lovers cannot be trusted to secure for boys the long-term advantages which were supposed to make paederastic affairs worthwhile. Socrates' first speech described the lover as a madman, distasteful and embarrassing in the short term, changeable and unreliable thereafter. In both cases the idea was that love itself interferes with paederasty, if the point of paederasty, as was widely assumed, was to socialize the boy into the life of a well-to-do Athenian citizen who was serious about his obligations toward his family, his friends, and his city.

Socrates' second speech looks far beyond such issues. Though love is still a madness, it is not the madness brought about when base desire overcomes reason (cf. 238b–c); rather, it is the result of the recollection of Beauty and of the other Forms which, however much we desire them, we cannot ever fully possess while we are still embodied. Love is a madness produced by an unsatisfiable rational desire to understand the ultimate truth about the world, prompted in the first instance by the desire to possess true Beauty. It is a madness sparked by a vision of truth and leading to its clearer apprehension; it is the madness of philosophy. *Erōs* is indispensable to paederasty because it provides the only entry into its real purpose: helping oneself and one's beloved to recall what the soul had seen in its travels around the heavens. And since that is the world of the Forms, which is the true object of knowledge, a good paederastic relationship is, for Plato, equivalent to the life of philosophy itself. The rewards of paederasty have nothing to do, as in the previous speeches, either with sexual pleasure or with worldly advantages; instead, they bring about a final liberation from "this thing we are carrying around now, which we call a body, locked in it like an oyster in its shell" (250c) and a return to the blissful existence of a well-balanced soul in its disembodied state.[19] Love moves the soul to the stars (cf. *Timaeus* 41e–42d).

It was important to give this brief outline of the views Plato has Socrates express in this speech, flat and inadequate as such an outline is bound to be, because so many of these views seem to correspond, as we have already said, to ideas Plato had presented in a number of dialogues earlier than the *Phaedrus*. Thus, the idea that *erōs* is really a mechanism of philosophy had already been presented in the *Symposium*. The theory that knowledge, particularly the knowledge of Forms, is recollection formed part of the *Meno* and the *Phaedo*. The theory of the divided soul, which was absent from the *Symposium*, became crucial in the *Republic*. The theory of Forms, introduced through an account of love and Beauty in the *Symposium*, was integral to the *Phaedo* and the *Republic*.[20] And the notion that the Form of Beauty is the most beautiful object in the world, the idea of "paradigmatism" according to which each Form is the perfect exemplar of the property for which it stands, is central to the metaphysics and epistemology of all these middle works. But in the *Phaedrus* these ideas are embedded in a highly rhetorical speech that Socrates will, in fact, later attempt to disown. A reading of the entire dialogue, therefore, must ask what attitude Plato is taking here toward the theories he had presented in these earlier works. This question is connected to the more general issue of the structure and unity of the *Phaedrus* as a whole.

Part Two: Discussion of Rhetoric and Writing (257b–279c)

The second part of the *Phaedrus* treats in dialogue form issues concerning the principles of rhetorical composition supposedly

---

19. Plato, we must remember, had already described philosophy in the *Phaedo* (64b–65d) as the mode of life closest to the life which the soul leads after death, free from body and sense.

20. On the relative dating of the *Symposium* and the *Phaedo*, see n. 42 below.

Introduction

raised by the speeches of the first. But the discussion addresses rhetoric in purely formal terms. Socrates and Phaedrus consider the proper composition of speeches, the knowledge that the good orator must possess, the relationship between rhetoric and philosophy, and the advantages and disadvantages of writing speeches in particular and of writing in general. *Erōs*, which was the subject of all three speeches and which assumed nothing less than cosmic importance in Socrates' Great Speech, is forgotten. How can we account for this strange fact?

That the second part of the *Phaedrus* is silent on *erōs* is strange, however, only if we assume that love is the *Phaedrus*' central topic. We have already said that this assumption has been often made, even by Plato's ancient readers, who gave the *Phaedrus* such subtitles as "Of the Beautiful" and "Of Love and of the Mind." But as Friedrich Schleiermacher observed as early as 1836, "the superadded titles of this dialogue . . . have been understood almost universally as indicating the true subject of it, have been translated and used in quotations, though love and beauty appear only in one part of the work, and could not, therefore, to an unprejudiced person, obtain as the true and proper subject of it."[21] And Schleiermacher goes on to argue, quite correctly, that not only is it impossible that the particular question of whether boys should favor men who do not love them over those who do could

> have been in Plato's mind the main-subject matter . . . but not even love in general. For in either case this beautiful work, worked up as it evidently is with the greatest pains, would appear deformed in a most revolting manner, utterly contravening the maxim that it must be fashioned like a living creature, having a body proportioned to the mind, with parts also in due proportion [cf. 264c]. For the whole of the second half would then be nothing but an appendage strangely tacked on, and not even tolerably well fitted. (p. 49)

Schleiermacher himself believes that the true subject-matter of the *Phaedrus* is philosophy itself and that the dialogue (which

---

21. Schleiermacher, *Introductions to the Dialogues of Plato*, p. 48.

he believed to be the first Plato ever composed)[22] is a blueprint for the philosophical edifice Plato already had in mind to construct. This is difficult to accept. What seems more reasonable, as we shall see in more detail below, is to suppose that the main subject of the dialogue is rhetoric—its nature, the proper way of pursuing it, if any, and its relation to philosophy. On such a reading, the three speeches that form its first part turn out to be examples Plato puts forward in order to support the conclusions he reaches in the second. Taking the speeches as examples of rhetorical structure explains why *erōs* does not appear in the subsequent discussion. Plato is more interested in what the speeches show about the practice of rhetoric than in what they reveal about the nature of love. But it also allows us to explain (as we must) why, among so many other possible subjects, Plato chose to compose his sample speeches on the topic of *erōs*. Neither their form nor their subject will appear random any longer.

Collectively, the speeches represent situations that were relatively common in the competitive atmosphere within which rhetoric grew in classical Athens.[23] If we take the first two, the speech of Lysias and Socrates' first effort, as a pair, we see that they both argue for a similar conclusion: Lovers are harmful. The two speeches represent a contest as to who, Lysias or Socrates/Plato, can compose a better speech on the very same topic. If, on the other hand, we group Socrates' two speeches together, we can see them as an instance of the commonplace fact that trained orators were able (and proud of their ability) to speak impressively on both sides of every issue. Does this then mean that

---

22. Schleiermacher places the *Phaedrus* first partly because he reads it as Plato's announcement of the nature and superiority of philosophy over other practices—a programmatic statement of his views in general. He also locates in it an "excessive, and almost boisterous and triumphant exultation," "an ostentation of power and superiority"; and he finds that its "spirit is youthful throughout" (pp. 59–62). His view of the dialogue's position in the sequence of Plato's dialogues is not entertained seriously by scholars today.

23. Note, for example, that when Phaedrus realizes that Socrates' second speech is intended as a praise of love, he promises that he will force Lysias to respond with a speech on that very subject (243d–e).

Socrates must believe that the two speeches are equally convincing? Not if we accept his own suggestion (262d, 265c–266a) that the two are really a single long oration, in which a bad kind of love is distinguished from a good kind. In that case, the speeches would only appear to give equal support to contradictory views; in reality they would be compatible with each other and both would contain a measure of truth, the first no less than the second.[24] Combining the speeches, and attributing to *erōs* a complexity beyond the farthest reaches of Lysias' imagination, thus gives Socrates an overall victory against his opponent.

But even if the speeches are formally connected with one another in these ways, the question of their subject still remains unanswered. If they are intended only as examples for the subsequent discussion of rhetoric, we need to ask why Plato chose *erōs* as his exemplary theme. Is his choice of love completely random? How could it be, given that it is a subject to which he had already attributed such crucial importance in the *Symposium* and which, in the *Phaedrus*, enables him to introduce so many of his views on other philosophical issues? But if it is not random, if Plato introduced it for some particular reason, what is his attitude toward the status of *erōs* and of those other issues? Why does Socrates not discuss them at all? Why does he take a dismissive tone toward his speech (cf. 262a–c, 265b–d)?

* * * * * * * * * * * *

We must now examine, again in very rough and general terms, the points regarding rhetoric that Plato makes in the second part of the dialogue.

Amazed at the beauty of Socrates' second speech, Phaedrus confesses that he is not sure Lysias could compose a better one. And he also adds that Lysias might be unwilling to continue the competition because he had recently been attacked on the grounds that speechwriting is a shameful occupation and not worthy of a gentleman's attention (257c). Socrates responds that writing speeches is not itself shameful; shame only attaches to composing speeches, orally or in written form, badly. So the

---

24. Socrates actually makes this point himself at 265e–266a.

question becomes when speeches are composed well and when not; and this is equivalent to asking when rhetoric is and when it is not correctly practiced. Instead of returning to Athens, the two friends decide to stay in the country and continue their discussion, on a philosophical level now, through the early afternoon. Socrates, in addition, points out the cicadas singing overhead. Consonant with the respect for myth and traditional theology which his visit to the countryside has produced in him, he describes the cicadas as the Muses' messengers. They are watching them, he says, and will report to the Muses whether the two friends have spent their time lazily drifting off in the summer heat or engaged in the sort of philosophical discussion that is a tribute to the cicadas' patron goddesses (258b–259e).[25]

Socrates begins the discussion by asking whether rhetoricians should always know the truth about their topics. Phaedrus offers the commonplace response that this is not at all necessary. Orators, he continues, need to know only what their *audience* considers to be just or good or noble, not what is really so (if anything is): it is by manipulating their audience's preconceived views, not by appealing to the actual truth, that rhetoricians succeed in convincing them of their own—the rhetoricians'—position (cf. *Gorgias* 452d). Conviction in this rhetorical context is connected to manipulation; what an audience already believes, whether or not it is true, allows them to be manipulated much more effectively than the actual truth, which they may well not believe at all.

Socrates responds by arguing at length that rhetoric can be pursued systematically, as a "craft" or "art" (*technē*),[26] only if

---

25. Ferrari, *Listening to the Cicadas*, builds his ambitious overall interpretation of the *Phaedrus* on a reading of this episode. His study is worth consulting on all the issues raised by this complex work.

26. The Greek word *technē*, often translated "art" in what follows, is actually quite different from that English word. It connotes, in contrast to our "art," a systematic body of knowledge which can be taught and which follows rather well formulated rules. We have kept, however, to the traditional rendering in our translation. An alternative translation might be "craft"; "science," which some translators prefer, is too strict a notion and corresponds more accurately to the Greek *epistēmē*.

Introduction

orators do actually know the truth about their subject. First he claims that orators who are ignorant of what is truly good or just may cause great harm to their audience. Second, he argues that only those who know precisely the truth about a subject can lead their audience, step by indiscernible step, away from their own beliefs and toward the conclusion they want by presenting arguments that diverge from that truth as little as possible. Only they know how least to diverge from the truth so as to be believable. In addition, their knowledge allows them to be aware when their opponents are in turn trying to mislead them and to resist them successfully: "If you are to deceive someone else and to avoid deception yourself, you must know precisely the respects in which things are similar and dissimilar to one another" (262a). Since knowledge of the truth is necessary for the ability to treat rhetoric systematically, and since Plato believes that the search for truth is philosophy, the main (and surprising) implication of Socrates' controversial argument is that finally only philosophers can be adequate rhetoricians (259e–262c).

Phaedrus and Socrates now turn to Lysias' speech in order to determine whether it has been composed systematically, as a result of *technē*, or haphazardly. It turns out that the speech proceeds by piling argument upon argument without concern for structure or for the relations among its various parts.[27] In

---

27. In contrast to Lysias', Socrates' own first speech proceeds in a very organized manner. After the definition of love, the speaker constructs the following sequence. He lists the bad effects of a lover on, first, the boy's mind; second, his body; and third, his possessions, family, and friends—that is, in descending order of importance. He then describes how unpleasant an older man's company is bound to be while he is still in love with the boy and goes on to anticipate the obnoxious behavior of such a man once the love affair is over. The conclusion lists these five points precisely in the reverse order from that in which they were presented, ending with what the speaker clearly considers most important, the harm lovers do to the souls of their beloved. According to the principle of composition enunciated at 264c, Socrates' speech is clearly superior to Lysias'. One might argue, however, that the latter is not at all haphazard, but that it is constructed in such a way that it will appear to be so and therefore informal and unstudied—as different from the usual supplications of other men toward boys as the speaker's unusual desires are from theirs.

particular, Socrates criticizes Lysias for beginning his speech without a definition of *erōs* that would allow the audience to have a clear idea of their topic (262d–264e).

Having established that speeches must be carefully constructed, Socrates now examines his own two efforts. Though he begins by treating them as independent works, he ends up thinking of them as one long speech divided into two parts. Their common element is that they both depend on a definition of *erōs* as madness, which they divide into two kinds—a bad one attacked in the first speech, and a good one praised in the second. Everything else in his speeches, Socrates now shockingly says, "was really a game." The only things that mattered were two: first, that the speeches collected all the phenomena that fall under *erōs* together and offered a general definition of that notion; second, that they divided madness, the genus to which *erōs* belongs, into its various kinds and finally located *erōs* itself within it, so as distinguish its bad aspect from its good, to criticize the former and celebrate the latter (265a–266b).

Such "collections and divisions," of which Socrates claims to be a lover (*erastēs*), turn out to be, in fact, the methods of dialectic, or philosophy.[28] So, the single serious idea that Socrates' two rhetorical speeches are supposed to illustrate is the practice of the method of philosophy. *Erōs* has disappeared altogether.[29] Philosophy, Socrates implies again, is necessary for the correct pursuit of rhetoric. But Phaedrus replies, quite correctly, that even though they may have succeeded in defining philosophy, rhetoric, which is after all their main topic, still eludes them (266c–d). For one thing, he claims, Socrates has left totally out of the picture all the many tropes and modes of argument that various teachers of rhetoric have identified in their handbooks.

---

28. Collection and division are the backbone of Plato's dialectical method in his late works. It is plausible to claim that they are presented here for the first time. They are practiced in detail in the *Sophist* and the *Statesman*. The *Philebus* discusses them in more general terms (14c–20c).

29. *Erōs* is mentioned in the discussion of collection and division, but only as the example on which the method was practiced. Nothing substantive is said about it.

Socrates, who turns out to have detailed knowledge of the technical aspects of rhetoric, responds that these can be of no help to a rhetorician who doesn't know how to put them together and how to utilize them in accordance with some general principles in order to construct acceptable speeches. Rhetoric requires much more than acquaintance with formal tricks (266d–269c).

What exactly, then, does rhetoric require in addition to its technical features? Socrates replies that as in the case of every *technē*, rhetoric must proceed through an understanding of the objects it involves. Rhetoric is a directing of the soul toward certain views and conclusions by means of speeches (261a, cf. 271c). Rhetoricians, therefore, must know the nature of the soul and its various kinds; they must also know the various kinds of speeches there are and how different souls are affected by them; and they must be able to detect the sort of soul they address in each particular case and therefore the kind of speech that is most appropriate to it. Only on the basis of such general understanding will the formal mechanisms classified by the various teachers of rhetoric find their place and fulfill their function (269d–272c).

We shall see that this grandiose conception of rhetoric, which actually places it so close to philosophy itself that the two may appear identical,[30] is important for answering our earlier question concerning the silence of the second part of the *Phaedrus* regarding *erōs*. For the moment, however, let us follow Socrates as he takes up a challenge to the conception of rhetoric he has just articulated. He imagines that one could object that the abstract study he has been recommending is quite useless to the practicing orator. According to this argument, which we have already encountered in the dialogue, the rhetorician only needs knowledge of what is plausible—what, that is, the audience will consider plausible in each particular case: the knowledge that rhetoric requires is practical and concrete; it concerns what people

---

30. The exact relationship between "true" rhetoric and philosophy is very difficult to determine. The question is discussed well, if not conclusively, in the debate between Christopher Rowe, "The Argument and Structure of Plato's *Phaedrus*," and Malcolm Heath, "The Unity of Plato's *Phaedrus*." Their interesting debate is continued in a series of responses, listed in the Bibliography.

believe to be true, not the truth itself. Truth has nothing to do with persuasion—only verisimilitude does. Socrates' response is that no one can know what is plausible without knowing what is true. After all, he claims, what is plausible is identical with what is likely to be the case; likeness to the truth is what makes something likely; and knowledge of the truth is therefore necessary in order to know what is likely and, for that reason, plausible (272c–274a).[31]

Rhetoric correctly conceived, therefore, requires knowledge of the truth about the subject of one's discourse. It also requires knowledge of the nature of the soul. It involves the ability to discern the kind of soul one is faced with in each particular case. And it also requires the ability to tell the truth in such a way that our audience, even if it is of limited ability, will be drawn toward it. The ornamentation which is an essential element of rhetoric is not directed at entertaining or manipulating an audience: its purpose is to bring that audience as close to the truth as it can get.

****

Having argued that rhetoric can be systematically practiced only by those who know the kinds of truths he has enumerated, Socrates turns to the question of when writing is and when it is not proper (274b–278e). This passage has received great attention in recent years, partly because of Jacques Derrida's influential interpretation of it as an attack on writing that necessarily undermines itself.[32] Derrida believes that Plato aims to argue that writing is in all cases inferior to oral communication. For Derrida, this is a general tendency of western philosophy, which, he argues, has tended to consider speech as a more direct, more comprehensible and less ambiguous mode of communication than writing. Speech is presumed to be clear, a direct expression of thought; and speakers can always explain their meaning if it

---

31. This argument, its weaknesses, and its immense influence on the rhetorical tradition are discussed by Cooper, "Plato, Isocrates and Cicero on the Independence of Oratory from Philosophy."
32. Derrida, "Plato's Pharmacy."

is misunderstood. Derrida, in a detailed reading of the passage to which we cannot do justice here, argues that Plato's attack fails in a peculiar way because, even as he tries to distinguish speech from writing, Plato needs to describe the former in terms of concepts and metaphors drawn from the latter. So, for example, Plato claims that speech, "the living, breathing discourse of the man who knows, of which the written one can be fairly called an image," is actually *"written down . . . in the soul of the listener"* (276a). But if speech has to be characterized in terms of writing, Derrida argues, speech itself must be characterized with the imperfections that attach to writing. What follows, he claims, is that there is no mode of communication which is free from misinterpretation, ambiguity, and appropriation by another person independently of its author's intentions. All the problems Plato identifies for writing apply to speech as well.

The interpretation of this passage is too complicated to discuss in any detail here, though it is well worth careful consideration in the course of reading the dialogue. Two alternative interpretations that deserve to be briefly mentioned are the following. One is that Plato is not here attacking all writing, but only a certain attitude toward it, an attitude which induces us to take for granted anything written, to refuse to question it, to consider it true, simply on the grounds that it has been written. But the same is true of oral discourse as well. Speech should no more be taken for granted than writing. Phaedrus may perhaps be willing to accept uncritically others' views, rhetorically or philosophically expressed, in speech or in writing. But in fact both speech and writing need to be questioned, put to the test, and made material for reflection. Socrates' strictures apply equally to speech and to writing so long as these are accepted as authoritative without first being examined in regard to their truth.[33]

A second, preferable, way of reading this passage is to claim that Plato's discussion is not essentially connected to the difference between speech and writing themselves. Though of course the discussion of the *Phaedrus* applies directly to speech and writing, it is a special case of a much more general debate,

---

33. This, greatly simplified, is the view of Ferrari, *Listening to the Cicadas*, pp. 214–222.

repeated over and over again, concerning the trustworthiness of a new and not yet understood mode of communication in comparison to that of an accepted medium. We generally tend to connect the older medium to rationality and to successful communication exclusively; we tend to describe the new one as less rational and much less likely to succeed in communicating ideas. What is often true in such discussions is that we make an unfair comparison: we judge the new medium according to its ability to communicate the type of ideas for which the older one had been designed, and it is no surprise that it fails in that regard. Moreover, we tend to identify the ideas suited to the old medium and the manner in which that medium communicates them with what is rational. Accordingly, even if the new medium is sometimes judged to be successful in communicating its own ideas by its own methods, we are tempted to consider these ideas at best as inferior to the former, at worst as irrational and harmful. For example, it is true, as Plato claims, that writing cannot answer questions in the way a speaker can in the course of a discussion. This is, from one point of view, a disadvantage of writing over speech. But speech cannot possibly communicate ideas that are as complex or textured as the ideas that can be expressed through a medium as permanent and as capable of review as writing. Each medium has its own advantages and disadvantages, and it is much more difficult than we often think to make a direct comparison between them. Nevertheless, we do. The general strategy for such comparisons is presented in the *Phaedrus* for the first time in western thought; speech and writing are simply the media of communication which were at issue at the time. But we can find its general form repeated again and again in the most different situations, with the same considerations applied to the most diverse examples. Its most recent instance is the negative comparison of the visual media, especially television, to writing. What is particularly ironic is that almost every argument Plato gave in the *Phaedrus* in favor of speech and against writing is now given in favor of writing and against television. This suggests that what matters in each specific case is not the pair of media being compared, but the fact that, having already accepted one medium as an effective and rational method of communication, we are bound to consider the other ineffective and unreasonable. We thus put the other

INTRODUCTION

medium at an inherent disadvantage from the very beginning, and we are prevented from taking its own claims seriously.[34]

At the end of their discussion of writing, Socrates tells Phaedrus that authors who write with a knowledge of the truth, able to defend their own works and aware that their writings are not themselves of great worth, should be considered philosophers. Those, on the other hand, whose main goal is to produce written texts without concern for the truth or for the shortcomings of their products should be considered rhetoricians or speech writers. Even in its written form, rhetoric can be part of the activity of philosophy provided that it is properly practiced (278c–e).

****

We now, finally, can turn directly to the complex question we could not answer without first having formed a general idea of the contents of the *Phaedrus*: Is this work unified? Do its two parts constitute elements in a single, coherent structure?

First, we must agree on what counts as unity in this context. Even this question is disputed. Malcolm Heath, for example, has made a strong case for thinking that the unity of the dialogue lies in its formal aspects, in the fact that though its two parts have radically different subjects, the work still satisfies Aristotle's criteria for having a unified plot.[35] Nevertheless, it would be

---

34. An egregious case of this type of argument can be found in Neil Postman's *Amusing Ourselves to Death* (New York: Viking, 1985). Postman simply applies Plato's argument regarding speech and writing to writing and television without any idea as to its origins. In this way he fails to appreciate, and to guard against, the irony of praising writing over the visual media for exactly the reasons Plato prefers speech to writing. See also Alexander Nehamas, "Plato and the Mass Media," *The Monist* 71 (1988): 214–234.

35. See Malcolm Heath, "The Unity of Plato's *Phaedrus*," who argues that the unity of the dialogue does not depend on a thematic connection between its two parts. He attributes to the work a "formal unity," a notion which he derives from Aristotle's discussion of the unity of drama in the *Poetics*. The unity of the *Phaedrus*, like the unity of a number of Greek plays, according to Heath, consists not in its addressing a single subject, but in the unity of its plot, which he construes as the fact that "the sequence of events that it narrates unfolds in accordance

more satisfying to show that the *Phaedrus* does after all address a single subject throughout and that its unity is not merely formal.

If the subject of the *Phaedrus* were *erōs*, it would be impossible, as we have seen, to find such a thematic unity in the work: *erōs* is simply not discussed in the dialogue's second part. But, as we have also seen, there is a subject that is central to every part of the work—rhetoric. We have already said that we need not read the *Phaedrus* as a treatise on *erōs* with an irrelevant, long discussion of rhetoric tagged on. We can read it instead as a sustained discussion of rhetoric in which Plato constructs three speeches on the topic of love as examples of what rhetoricians are capable of doing and as objects of criticism or praise.

Such a view immediately explains the formal relations we noted above among the three speeches of the *Phaedrus* (pp. xxvi–xxvii). In a discussion of rhetoric, it makes sense to portray the competitive situations in which rhetoricians found themselves in the course of practicing their profession. But our approach generates two new questions. The first is why Plato chooses *erōs* as the subject of his exemplary speeches. If *erōs* were itself the dialogue's central subject (or even, as Heath argues, one of two subjects addressed in the work), this question would not have to be raised. But our reading implies that Plato could have composed the dialogue's speeches on any topic that could be addressed by rhetoric; why, among such a large range, did he decide on *erōs*? The second question concerns the status of the speeches, especially the status of the Great Speech. This, in turn, can be broken down into two further problems. First, the Great Speech, like the rest of the *Phaedrus*, is in fact a written discourse and therefore subject to Plato's objections against writing. Even though, within the dialogue's fiction, it is spoken by Socrates, and not written in the way that Lysias' speech has been written down, it is (along with the whole dialogue) a piece of writing as far as Plato's readers are concerned. What, then, does Plato think of the speech's contents? What, indeed, does he think of the whole of the *Phaedrus*? Second, even within the fiction of the dialogue, in which Socrates delivers it orally, the speech

---

with necessity and probability; given these people in this situation, that is indeed what they would do and say" (p. 161).

INTRODUCTION xxxix

is a work of rhetoric, and must fall short of the accuracy that philosophy (and only philosophy) possesses in Plato's eyes. The speech is long and of great beauty, and it presents views that have been central to Plato's philosophy. But can Plato believe its contents in view of its inferior status?

Let us first consider Plato's choice of *erōs* as the subject of the speeches of the *Phaedrus*. Plato had already addressed *erōs* rhetorically in the *Symposium*, and he may well have thought it an appropriate subject for this discussion of rhetoric—all the more if he has changed some of his views on *erōs* in the meantime. And it seems clear that, on some issues at least, Plato has in fact changed his mind. The *Phaedrus*, for example, depends crucially on the notion of the divided soul, which Plato first introduced in the *Republic* and which accounts for the difficulty that lovers have in controlling their sexual appetites even after they have begun to realize that love is primarily directed not toward sex but toward philosophy. By contrast, the *Symposium* does not appeal to such a divided soul. An undivided soul, all of it always desiring what it considers best, is subject to no such conflicts. It cannot possibly be tempted by desires for the body once it has determined that the soul is more beautiful and therefore worthier of love. And according to the *Symposium*, lovers desire the higher objects of love as soon as they become aware of their existence: leaving their earlier loves behind, those who can see far enough progress toward true love, which is love of the Form of Beauty (*Symposium* 210a–211b2).[36]

---

36. Dorothea Frede, in "Out of the Cave: What Socrates Learned from Diotima," *Nomodeiktes* (1993), argues that the fact that the divided soul is not mentioned in the *Symposium* does not show that this dialogue was written before the *Republic*. Plato, she claims, only uses the divided soul when he needs it, and so we can draw no conclusions from his silence regarding it in the *Symposium* (p. 403, n. 15). But note that, as we have just argued, the theory of the divided soul makes a big difference to how *erōs* is presented in the *Symposium* and in the *Phaedrus*. Plato, in other words, should have used the theory of the divided soul if it was available to him when he was composing the former dialogue. Other differences between the two works can also be detected, though they are not quite so many nor are they so obviously connected with general conclusions about

Plato may have had a second reason for considering *erōs* an appropriate subject. Precisely because he believes that it is a force that moves the soul to the Forms and to philosophy, he can use it in order to introduce various philosophical views that might otherwise not easily have found a place within the dialogue. *Erōs* provides an entry into the heart of Plato's philosophy.

Finally, we might consider the following possibility. The best way to persuade people to devote themselves to philosophy is by showing them what philosophy is and what benefits they can derive from it. But most of us lack the knowledge, or the kind of soul, that can respond directly to the dry and technical collections and divisions of which Socrates, for one, is a lover. For those without the right soul, love for another human being, which is a phenomenon many come to know at some time or other during their lifetime, may be as close as they will get to the philosophical life—*erōs* knows how to awaken souls and give them wings, raising them from the deathlike condition which is what Plato believes life on earth is. *Erōs* is the only force that will "direct the soul" of most of us, and especially the soul of Phaedrus as he is portrayed in this dialogue. And that is another reason why it is a perfect subject for the speeches through a discussion of which Plato tries to distinguish rhetoric from philosophy.[37]

But this now brings us to the second question we asked above: Can Plato be serious about the views he expresses in Socrates' Great Speech? Socrates himself characterizes his speech as "playful"— though, to be accurate, he also says that it is "appropriate and respectful" (265b–c). But without such a rhetorical exhortation (and, in many cases, even with it), the mere experience of *erōs* would surely not prove enough to move those who have it toward philosophy: its rewards are most often pursued in other

---

Plato's life and philosophical development as Martha Nussbaum, for example, claims in *The Fragility of Goodness*, ch. 7.

37. The connection between *erōs* and persuasion (*peithō*) is an old one in Greek thought: desire is compelling, like a powerful speech. It is even reported that Sappho had written that Persuasion was the daughter of Aphrodite. See Campbell, *Greek Lyric*; Sappho, fragments 90 and 200; and the Appendix.

INTRODUCTION

directions. Does Plato, though, believe the content of his rhetorical effort, when in the second part of his dialogue he takes such pains to separate rhetoric from philosophy? If even true rhetoricians cannot speak the plain truth but must embellish it so as to make it attractive and convincing to their audience on each particular occasion, how much of the Great Speech is true and how much of it is, so to speak, an inflection of the truth produced for Phaedrus' benefit?

At 277b–c, Socrates claims that true rhetoricians will have to understand the method of collection and division which they will apply both to their topics and to the souls of their listeners. This enables them to give the speech that is appropriate on each occasion, "a complex and elaborate speech to a complex and elaborate soul and a simple speech to a simple one." The knowledge Socrates attributes to the true rhetorician here (cf. 271c–272c) is at least in part the knowledge he has earlier attributed to the dialectician or philosopher (265c–266c). In other words, whatever exactly the relationship is between "true rhetoric" and philosophy, a true rhetorician will know how best to bring an audience as close to the truth as it is possible for them to come in view of their abilities.

Phaedrus is not a philosopher's ideal listener; his soul is not "simple" but "complex and elaborate." The "mythical" speech in praise of *erōs*, therefore, must have been designed especially for him and for his interests. It is thus an example of true rhetoric, spoken by someone who knows the truth but has tailored his presentation to his listener's character. Socrates' speech does not therefore present the unadorned truth about philosophy or the theory of Forms. It is an artful construction which inflects the truth in order to appeal to Phaedrus' specific needs and abilities. This is an important reason, incidentally, why we should not assume without further argument that Plato is prepared to defend the views expressed in the speech in just the form he presents them here: they need not be, and almost certainly are not, the truth just as Plato sees it.

This point has been appreciated by recent readers of the *Phaedrus*.[38] But a question that has not been given enough attention

---

38. See again the essays by Rowe and Heath referred to above.

is this: Let us suppose that the Great Speech does inflect the truth; which part of it is the truth and which the inflection? Is there a distinct part that Plato himself believes more or less literally and another that he composes for Phaedrus' sake? The most obvious answer, and the answer given or presupposed in most discussions of the *Phaedrus*, is that Plato believes in the theory of Forms, in the doctrine of the divided soul, in the theory of recollection, in the transmigration of the soul—in all the theories, that is, that the speech contains. Accordingly, the inflection consists in his vivid mythological imagery, especially the story of the soul as a winged chariot traveling in the company of the gods and of its fate.

But this view runs into a serious problem: We have good reason to think that by the time he wrote the *Phaedrus*, Plato no longer accepted the theory of Forms as it is presented in the Great Speech. The method of collection and division, which is described as the method of philosophy in the dialogue's second part, goes hand in hand with the theory of Forms as we find it in Plato's later dialogues, particularly the *Sophist* and the *Philebus*.[39] But that theory is obviously not the same as the theory of Forms we find in Plato's middle works, especially the *Phaedo* and the *Republic*. This middle theory was subjected to serious criticisms in the *Parmenides*, and its paradigmatism was particularly put to the test. Paradigmatism consists in the idea that each Form is the perfect exemplar of the feature for which it stands: Beauty, for instance, is the most beautiful object in the world; Largeness, the largest. This idea, of course, is at the heart of Socrates' Great Speech. If Beauty were not itself beautiful, there

---

39. In his discussion of the similarities between rhetoric and medicine, Socrates at one point (270c–d) says that in order to understand the nature of anything we must know what capacity that object has of acting on and being acted upon by what other things in the world. The idea here is identical to the "criterion" or "definition" (*horos*) of what it is to be that Plato attributes to the Eleatic Stranger in the *Sophist* (247d–e). The view that such "dynamic" relations constitute the nature of real objects contrasts seriously with the notion that the Forms cannot be affected by other things, which seems presupposed in the middle dialogues and is criticized at length in the *Parmenides*.

would be no reason for the soul to recollect it upon seeing a beautiful boy. And if the Form were not supremely beautiful—much more beautiful than the boy—there would be no reason to be drawn toward it instead of remaining solely in love with the boy.

Another feature of the middle theory of Forms is that it is not at all clear that it allows the Forms to be related to one another. Each Form is complete in itself, its nature independent of everything else (see *Symposium* 211a–b); Plato often describes our coming to know the Forms, as he does in the *Phaedrus*, by metaphors drawn from sight. Such metaphors reinforce the notion that each Form is an independent object which can be seen in its entirety by itself. But the theory of Forms of the Great Speech is incompatible with the theory the second part of the dialogue implies. The method of collection and division depends on the idea that the Forms are closely connected with one another and that to know a Form is to know its connections: to divide a Form (itself an impossible task according to the middle theory attacked in the *Parmenides*, which asserts that each Form is indivisible) is to determine the Forms to which it is related as a genus is related to its species. According to the late dialogues, the Forms constitute a great network of essentially interrelated objects. And this is not at all the picture of the Great Speech. The Forms of the middle theory are, as the *Parmenides* insists, "separate" both from each other and from their many instances. There is no way to account for the relation, if any, between the Forms and their instances (*Parmenides* 130b–134e). But when the *Philebus* discusses collection and division it leaves us with an impression at least that the connections between the world of Forms and the world of sensible objects are much more intimate. Division of a Form, for example, may end precisely when we reach the countless objects that fall under it.[40]

The theory of Forms is not the only obstacle to claiming that Plato accepts the views of the Great Speech in their literal form. The fact is that most of these views do not appear in Plato's later

---

40. See Dorothea Frede, *Plato: "Philebus"* (Indianapolis: Hackett Publishing Company, 1993), pp. xx–xxx, for a good discussion of this very complex problem.

work. For example, after his dramatic presentation of the theory of recollection—which had been so crucial to the *Meno* and the *Phaedo*—in the Great Speech of the *Phaedrus*, Plato simply never appeals to it again: not, for example, in the *Theaetetus*, which is explicitly devoted to establishing the nature of knowledge. Further, though the doctrine of the tripartite soul does reappear in the *Timaeus*, it does so in significantly different form. While all three parts of the soul are immortal in the Great Speech, only reason defies death in the *Timaeus*.[41]

What, then, if we were to turn our usual picture of the Great Speech around? What if we were to think that the truth Plato accepts does not consist of the philosophical theories the speech contains? What if Plato simply wants to communicate instead the idea that philosophy is the most important part of life? In that case, the theories of the speech, which Socrates presents so colorfully, will turn out to be the means by which he tries to move Phaedrus to realize that philosophy is superior to a life that finds its greatest pleasures in rhetoric. It is not clear that Socrates is perfectly successful in his effort, but at least Phaedrus is willing to continue their conversation into the afternoon instead of returning to the city, in order to persuade Lysias to compose a hymn to *erōs* that will outdo Socrates' own (257c). If only for a short while, Phaedrus actually *engages* in philosophy with Socrates.

The countryside, for which Socrates has left Athens, has turned him, surprisingly, into an accomplished rhetorician. Much more surprisingly, however, it has provided him with an opportunity to cast doubt on views that, within the fiction of Plato's dialogues, he had developed within the city walls. This Odysseus returns home from abroad a different man indeed.

If we suppose that Plato makes Socrates present picturesque views of Forms and souls to delight Phaedrus and to direct his soul toward philosophy, we can draw a further conclusion. Since Plato treats these theories no longer as ends in themselves but

---

41. All three parts of the soul are immortal, as far as we can tell, in the *Republic* as well. There is no indication here, as there is in the *Timaeus* (41d–42d, 69d–72d), that the two lower parts are mortal and accrue to the soul simply because it is incarnated.

INTRODUCTION

as means, we can now read Socrates' Great Speech as Plato's farewell to the theory of Forms it describes. What the speech shows is that the middle theory of Forms is as good as a good story—good enough to lead some people to philosophy, and perhaps even good enough to have led Plato himself to it. But once you do get there—really there—you realize that philosophy consists in the austere practice of collection and division, defining the kinds of things there are and distinguishing each from everything else. The theory of Forms as we came to know it in Plato's middle works has had its use; and it may still have an important role to play in firing the imagination. In fact, it has played just that role during a great part of the history of western philosophy: generations of readers, reading the speech as Phaedrus is supposed to have listened to it, have turned to philosophy because of the beauty of the vision of Plato's middle theory of Forms; not many have ended up believing it.

It might seem strange that Plato would produce such a beautiful piece of prose in order to part company with his own views. But the beauty of the speech makes the parting all that more moving. The *Phaedrus* is not simply discarding a rusted tool that has outlived its usefulness. It is leaving behind a set of views that had led to the most valuable form human life can take; without such views such a life could not have been articulated in the first place. Socrates' Great Speech exudes gratitude for what first made that life possible. It is a farewell to a dying friend; but its beauty has secured that friend an undying afterlife. And since Plato first introduced the Forms, in the *Symposium*, through a speech on *erōs* (210e–212b), nothing would have been more appropriate than to have taken leave of them through a speech on the same topic.[42] *Erōs* is literally the beginning and

---

42. This argument presupposes that the *Symposium* was written before the *Phaedo*. The issue is murky, and there is no external evidence to decide it. On internal grounds, it seems plausible to date the *Symposium* first: it envisages an undivided agent, very much as the earlier *Protagoras* does and in contrast to the divided agent (composed of body and soul, each a source of motivation in its own right) of the *Phaedo* and the divided soul of the *Republic*; in addition, the *Symposium*'s portrait of Socrates is much more consonant with that of Plato's early dialogues than with the otherworldly picture so starkly painted in the *Phaedo*.

the end of the theory of Forms of Plato's middle dialogues, and the *Phaedrus* is Plato's valedictory address to it.

The *Phaedrus* is thus a companion piece to the *Parmenides*. Both dialogues, in extremely different ways, leave the middle theory of Forms behind. Both emphasize that the activity of philosophy is more important than the specific views one holds. This is, according to our reading, the main thrust of Socrates' Great Speech. Similarly, Parmenides claims that even if the theory of Forms as Socrates had presented it is indefensible, some version of it is necessary if dialectic is to be at all possible (135b–c). Philosophy in general—not the literal content of any particular philosophical theory—constitutes in both cases the primary concern.

If Plato does not literally believe the philosophical theories of the Great Speech, does this mean that the speech cannot help us determine his views? Is there no point in reading it for information on Plato's substantive doctrines? There is. Even if Plato no longer accepts the theory of Forms in the version contained in the Great Speech, this does not imply that he was not earlier himself devoted to what is here primarily an artifice to move Phaedrus to philosophy. There is no reason to believe that the theory of Forms in the *Phaedrus* is not, at least to some extent, an accurate rendition of what he himself considered his earlier views to have been. The Great Speech can give us important information about the philosophy of the *Symposium*, the *Phaedo*, and the *Republic*.

But the *Phaedrus* is a written work, and we have seen that Plato has warned his readers not to put much trust in writing. What, then, should our own attitude toward the dialogue be? What should we believe of what we read here? Plato himself writes that written texts cannot be taken very seriously; writings that are recited without giving their audience the opportunity to question them and learn from them produce only conviction and not knowledge (277e). Perhaps, then, the *Phaedrus* itself, like all of Plato's texts and like all the rhetorical works to which he assimilates writing, should not be taken too seriously? Perhaps the whole dialogue, like the speeches in it, is itself a "game"?

But what does it mean to avoid taking the *Phaedrus* seriously? It does not mean that we are to consider it simply as a long joke.

It means that, like rhetoric, the dialogue also cannot produce knowledge but only conviction.[43] But, unlike rhetoric, it can still be questioned, because, like so many others of Plato's works, it leaves its own questions unanswered. To question the *Phaedrus*, therefore, is to continue asking its questions. Asking its questions, questioning the answers we give them, and even disputing the interpretation of Socrates' Great Speech given here, are, of course, doing philosophy. And so, not to take the *Phaedrus* seriously in the proper sense is to take philosophy itself seriously. But to take philosophy seriously, perhaps paradoxically but also appropriately for a work that delights in paradoxes and twists of its own, is to take the *Phaedrus* as well very seriously after all.

---

43. Cf. Rowe, "The Argument and Structure of Plato's *Phaedrus*," p. 120.

OUTLINE OF THE *PHAEDRUS*

1. Introduction, scene-setting: 227A–230E
2. Lysias' speech: 230E–234C
3. Socrates' challenge to Lysias: 234C–237B
4. Socrates' first speech: 237B–241D
5. Socrates' recantation of his first speech: 241D–243E
6. Socrates' second speech: 243E–257B
7. Transition to discussion of rhetoric: 257B–259D
8. Discussion of rhetoric: 259E–274B
9. Discussion of writing: 274B–277A
10. Conclusion: 277A–279C

PHAEDRUS

SOCRATES. PHAEDRUS, MY FRIEND! Where have you 227A
been? And where are you going?
PHAEDRUS. I was with Lysias, the son of Cephalus,[1] Socrates, and I am going for a walk outside the city walls because I was with him for a long time, sitting there the whole morning. You see, I'm keeping in mind the advice of our mutual friend Acumenus,[2] who says it's more refreshing to walk 227B along country roads than city streets.
So. He is quite right, too, my friend. So Lysias, I take it,[3] is in the city?
PH. Yes, at the house of Epicrates, which used to belong to Morychus,[4] near the temple of the Olympian Zeus.

---

1. Cephalus was prominent in the opening section of Plato's *Republic*, which is set in his home in Piraeus, the port of Athens. He had come there from Syracuse and was successful in the manufacture of shields. His sons Lysias, Polemarchus, and Euthydemus were known for their democratic sympathies. Polemarchus, who was interested in philosophy (cf. 257b4) and is shown taking an active part in the discussion of the *Republic*, was killed by the Thirty Tyrants. After the restoration of democracy, Lysias (ca.459–ca.380) was given the rights of a citizen of Athens.

2. Acumenus, a relative of the doctor Eryximachus who speaks in the *Symposium*, was a doctor himself (*Protagoras* 315c; see the exchange between Phaedrus and Eryximachus in *Symposium* 176b–e).

3. "I take it": *hōs eoiken*. The Greek verb is directly related to *to eikos*, "what is likely," "what is plausible," "what seems to be the case." Since *to eikos* is the main notion to which rhetoricians such as Lysias appeal in their speeches, Plato's use of this expression here and elsewhere in the dialogue is not accidental. We have tried to translate instances of these terms and their derivatives with expressions involving the notions of "likeness" and what is "likely," though this has not always been possible. For more discussion of *to eikos*, cf n. 170 below.

4. Morychus is mentioned on a number of occasions by Aristophanes for his luxurious ways.

So. What were you doing there? Oh, I know: Lysias must have been entertaining you with a feast of eloquence.

Ph. You'll hear about it, if you are free to come along and listen.

So. What? Don't you think I would consider it "more important than the most pressing engagement," as Pindar says, to hear how you and Lysias spent your time?[5]

Ph. Lead the way, then.

So. If only you will tell me.

Ph. In fact, Socrates, you're just the right person to hear the speech that occupied us, since, in a roundabout way, it was about love. It is aimed at seducing a beautiful boy, but the speaker is not in love with him—this is actually what is so clever and elegant about it: Lysias argues that it is better to give your favors to someone who does not love you than to someone who does.

So. What a wonderful man! I wish he would write that you should give your favors to a poor rather than to a rich man, to an older rather than to a younger one—that is, to someone like me and most other people: then his speeches would be really sophisticated, and they'd contribute to the public good besides! In any case, I am so eager to hear it that I would follow you even if you were walking all the way to Megara, as Herodicus recommends, to touch the wall and come back again.[6]

Ph. What on earth do you mean, Socrates? Do you think that a mere dilettante like me could recite from memory in a manner worthy of him a speech that Lysias, the best of our writers, took such time and trouble to compose? Far from it—though actually I would rather be able to do that than come into a large fortune!

So. Oh, Phaedrus, if I don't know my Phaedrus I must be forgetting who I am myself—and neither is the case.[7] I know very

---

5. Pindar, *Isthmian* I.2, adapted by Plato.

6. Herodicus was a medical expert whose regimen Socrates criticizes in *Republic* 406a–b.

7. Socrates' speech (228a–c) parodies the style of courtroom oratory, from his opening appeal to impossibility to his prosecution-style version

INTRODUCTION

well that he did not hear Lysias' speech only once: he asked him to repeat it over and over again, and Lysias was eager to oblige. But not even that was enough for him. In the end, he took the book himself and pored over the parts he liked 228B best. He sat reading all morning long, and when he got tired, he went for a walk, having learned—I am quite sure—the whole speech by heart, unless it was extraordinarily long. So he started for the country, where he could practice reciting it. And running into a man who is sick with passion for hearing speeches, seeing him—just seeing him—he was filled with delight: he had found a partner for his frenzied dance, and he urged him to lead the way.[8] But when that lover of speeches asked him to recite it, he played coy and 228C pretended that he did not want to. In the end, of course, he was going to recite it even if he had to force an unwilling audience to listen. So, please, Phaedrus, beg him to do it right now. He'll do it soon enough anyway.

PH. Well, I'd better try to recite it as best I can: you'll obviously not leave me in peace until I do so one way or another.

So. You are absolutely right.

PH. That's what I'll do, then. But, Socrates, it really is true that 228D I did not memorize the speech word for word; instead, I will give a careful summary of its general sense, listing all the ways he said the lover differs from the non-lover, in the proper order.

So. Only if you first show me what you are holding in your left hand under your cloak, my friend. I strongly suspect you have the speech itself. And if I'm right, you can be sure that,

---

of events. In the manner of Tisias (273a, below) Socrates rests his case on what is likely (*eikos*).

8. "His frenzied dance": Socrates refers to the rites of the Corybantes, who danced themselves into an ecstatic state. Such allusions to ecstasy-producing religious practices are common in the *Phaedrus*. Cf. 234d (Bacchic frenzy), 241e (possession by Nymphs), 244b and 248d–e (ecstasy of the oracles), 245a and 262d (possession by the Muses), and 250b–d (the ultimate vision after initiation into a cult). Cf. the language of initiation throughout Diotima's speech in the *Symposium*.

228E though I love you dearly, I'll never, as long as Lysias himself is present, allow you to practice your own speechmaking on me. Come on, then, show me.

PH. Enough, enough. You've dashed my hopes of using you as my training partner, Socrates. All right, where do you want to sit while we read?

229A SO. Let's leave the path here and walk along the Ilisus; then we can sit quietly wherever we find the right spot.

PH. How lucky, then, that I am barefoot today—you, of course, are always so. The easiest thing to do is to walk right in the stream; this way, we'll also get our feet wet, which is very pleasant, especially at this hour and season.

SO. Lead the way, then, and find us a place to sit.

PH. Do you see that very tall plane tree?[9]

SO. Of course.

229B PH. It's shady, with a light breeze; we can sit or, if we prefer, lie down on the grass there.

SO. Lead on, then.

PH. Tell me, Socrates, isn't it from somewhere near this stretch of the Ilisus that people say Boreas carried Oreithuia away?[10]

SO. So they say.

PH. Couldn't this be the very spot? The stream is lovely, pure and clear: just right for girls to be playing nearby.

229C SO. No, it is two or three hundred yards farther downstream, where one crosses to get to the district of Agra.[11] I think there is even an altar to Boreas there.

PH. I hadn't noticed it. But tell me, Socrates, in the name of Zeus, do you really believe that that legend is true?

SO. Actually, it would not be out of place for me to reject it, as our intellectuals do. I could then tell a clever story: I could

---

9. A plane tree is a European sycamore or buttonwood tree.

10. According to legend, Oreithuia, daughter of the Athenian king Erechtheus, was abducted by Boreas while she was playing with Nymphs along the banks of the Ilisus River. Boreas personifies the north wind.

11. One of the demes of classical Athens.

Introduction

claim that a gust of the North Wind blew her over the rocks where she was playing with Pharmaceia; and once she was killed that way people said she had been carried off by Boreas—or was it, perhaps, from the Areopagus?[12] The story is also told that she was carried away from there instead. Now, Phaedrus, such explanations are amusing enough, but they are a job for a man I cannot envy at all. He'd have to be far too ingenious and work too hard—mainly because after that he will have to go on and give a rational account of the form of the Hippocentaurs, and then of the Chimaera; and a whole flood of Gorgons and Pegasuses and other monsters, in large numbers and absurd forms, will overwhelm him.[13] Anyone who does not believe in them, who wants to explain them away and make them plausible by means of some sort of rough ingenuity, will need a great deal of time.

229D

229E

But I have no time for such things; and the reason, my friend, is this. I am still unable, as the Delphic inscription orders, to know myself; and it really seems to me ridiculous to look into other things before I have understood that.[14] This is why I do not concern myself with them. I accept what is generally believed, and, as I was just saying, I look not into them but into my own self: Am I a beast more complicated and savage than Typho,[15] or am I a tamer, sim-

230A

---

12. "The Hill of Ares (god of war)," located northwest of the Acropolis; it was, from very ancient times, the seat of a civic council which was itself called "Areopagus."
13. Demythologizing such accounts will not be easy: a Hippocentaur is half man, half horse; the Chimaera has a lion's head, goat's body, and serpent's tail; a Gorgon was a woman with snakes for hair; and Pegasus was a winged horse. Socrates is about to invent his own such figure, the winged team and chariot driver which we meet in his second speech below.
14. "To know myself": The famous stone at Delphi read "Know thyself" on one side and "Nothing in excess" on the other. Cf. *Apology* 38a, "the unexamined life is not worth living for a human being."
15. Typho is a fabulous multiform beast with a hundred heads resembling many different animal species. Plato puns on its name when he has Socrates say that he might have a "gentle" nature. The Greek word here is *atuphos*, which could be taken literally as meaning "un-Typho-

230B   PH. That's the one.

       SO. By Hera,[16] it really is a beautiful resting place. The plane tree is tall and very broad; the chaste-tree, high as it is, is wonderfully shady, and since it is in full bloom, the whole place is filled with its fragrance.[17] From under the plane tree the loveliest spring runs with very cool water—our feet can testify to that. The place appears to be dedicated to Achelous and some of the Nymphs, if we can judge from the statues

230C   and votive offerings.[18] Feel the freshness of the air; how pretty and pleasant it is; how it echoes with the summery, sweet song of the cicadas' chorus! The most exquisite thing of all, of course, is the grassy slope: it rises so gently that you can rest your head perfectly when you lie down on it. You've really been the most marvelous guide, my dear Phaedrus.

       PH. And you, my remarkable friend, appear to be totally out of place. Really, just as you say, you seem to need a guide,

230D   not to be one of the locals. Not only do you never travel abroad—as far as I can tell, you never even set foot beyond the city walls.

       SO. Forgive me, my friend. I am devoted to learning; landscapes and trees have nothing to teach me—only the people in the city can do that. But you, I think, have found a potion to charm me into leaving. For just as people lead hungry ani-

230E   mals forward by shaking branches of fruit before them, you

---

like." See Hesiod, *Theogony* 820 ff., and cf. Plato's use of such an image at *Republic* 588c ff.

16. "By Hera" is a common oath of Socrates.

17. The chaste-tree (Greek *agnos*) was associated with the notion of chastity because of the similarity between its name and the word for "chaste" (*hagnos*).

18. Achelous is a river god. The Nymphs are benevolent female deities associated with natural phenomena such as streams, woods, and mountains.

LYSIAS' SPEECH can lead me all over Attica or anywhere else you like simply by waving in front of me the leaves of a book containing a speech. But now, having gotten as far as this place this time around, I intend to lie down; so choose whatever position you think will be most comfortable for you, and read on.

PH. Listen, then:[19]

"You understand my situation: I've told you how good it would be for us, in my opinion, if this worked out. In any case, I don't think I should lose the chance to get what I am asking for,[20] merely because I don't happen to be in love with you.

231A

"A man in love will wish he had not done you any favors once his desire dies down, but the time will never come for a man who's not in love to change his mind. That is because the favors he does for you are not forced but voluntary; and he does the best that he possibly can for you, just as he would for his own business.

---

19. Is this speech a genuine speech by Lysias, or did Plato create it as a parody of Lysias' opinions and style? The question is very difficult to answer, and opinion is divided among scholars (see Dover, *Lysias and the Corpus Lysiacum*, pp. 69–71). Plato writes well in many styles, so he could well have written this himself, as a work of historical fiction. The most plausible hypothesis is that it is Plato's creation—and thus characteristic of his usual practice; consider, for example, Protagoras' "Great Speech" in the *Protagoras* (320d–328d) or Diotima's speech in the *Symposium* (203b–212c), both of which were almost certainly composed by Plato himself.

The speech plays on expectations about *erōs* which are well established in Greek literature (see Appendix). *Erōs*, as we find it in the *Phaedrus*, is the sexual desire an older man feels for a younger one, a passion that strikes the lover as a debilitating sickness or madness. By contrast, *philia*, often translated as "friendship," is mutual love between friends or family members; it is not accompanied by sexual desire, is not experienced as madness, and is never annoying to either party.

Noteworthy features of the speech are the speaker's reluctance to mention sex directly, his pretense that he is not a lover when he plainly wants sexual favors from the boy, and his consistent praise of friendship. His predictions about the behavior of lovers are examples of reasoning from "what is likely" (*eikos*), on which see 273a.

20. "What I am asking for": sex.

231B "Besides, a lover keeps his eye on the balance sheet—where his interests have suffered from love, and where he has done well; and when he adds up all the trouble he has taken, he thinks he's long since given the boy he loved a fair return. A non-lover, on the other hand, can't complain about love's making him neglect his own business; he can't keep a tab on the trouble he's been through, or blame you for the quarrels he's had with his relatives. Take away all those headaches and there's nothing left for him to do but put his heart into whatever he thinks will give pleasure.[21]

231C "Besides, suppose a lover does deserve to be honored because, as they say, he is the best friend his loved one will ever have, and he stands ready to please his boy with all those words and deeds that are so annoying to everyone else. It's easy to see (if he is telling the truth) that the next time he falls in love he will care more for his new love than for the old one, and it's clear he'll treat the old one shabbily whenever that will please the new one.

231D "And anyway, what sense does it make to throw away something like that[22] on a person who has fallen into such a miserable condition that those who have suffered it don't even try to defend themselves against it?[23] A lover will admit that he's more sick than sound in the head. He's well aware that he is not thinking straight; but he'll say he can't get himself under control. So when he does start thinking straight, why would he stand by decisions he had made when he was sick?

---

21. "Whatever he thinks will give pleasure": To whom? The speaker leaves it open whether the pleasure is to be his or the boy's. We have left the pronoun in the Greek untranslated because its reference is uncertain.
22. "What sense does it make": Literally, "Is it likely (*eikos*) that"; similar expressions occur at 232a, 232c, and 233a below. On *eikos* see 272e, ff. "Something like that": sex.
23. "Who has fallen into such a miserable condition": who has fallen in love. The seriousness of the disease is shown by the fact that those who have had it cannot summon up the will to fight against it or to resist a recurrence of the infection.

"Another point: if you were to choose the best of those who are in love with you, you'd have a pretty small group to pick from; but you'll have a large group if you don't care whether he loves you or not and just pick the one who suits you best; and in that larger pool you'll have a much better hope of finding someone who deserves your friendship. *231E*

"Now suppose you're afraid of conventional standards and the stigma that will come to you if people find out about this. Well, it stands to reason that a lover—thinking that everyone else will admire him for his success as much as he *232A* admires himself—will fly into words and proudly declare to all and sundry that his labors were not in vain. Someone who does not love you, on the other hand, can control himself and will choose to do what is best, rather than seek the glory that comes from popular reputation.

"Besides, it's inevitable that a lover will be found out: many people will see that he devotes his life to following the boy he loves. The result is that whenever people see you talking with him they'll think you are spending time together *232B* just before or just after giving way to desire. But they won't even begin to find fault with people for spending time together if they are not lovers; they know one has to talk to someone, either out of friendship or to obtain some other pleasure.

"Another point: have you been alarmed by the thought that it is hard for friendships to last? Or that when people break up, it's ordinarily just as awful for one side as it is for the other, but when you've given up what is most important *232C* to you already,[24] then your loss is greater than his? If so, it would make more sense for you to be afraid of lovers. For a lover is easily annoyed, and whatever happens, he'll think it was designed to hurt him. That is why a lover prevents the boy he loves from spending time with other people. He's afraid that wealthy men will outshine him with their money, while men of education will turn out to have the advantage of greater intelligence. And he watches like a hawk everyone who may have any other advantage over him! Once he's *232D*

---

24. "What is most important to you": sex.

persuaded you to turn those people away, he'll have you completely isolated from friends; and if you show more sense than he does in looking after your own interests, you'll come to quarrel with him.

"But if a man really does not love you, if it is only because of his excellence that he got what he asked for, then he won't be jealous of the people who spend time with you. Quite the contrary! He'll hate anyone who does not want to be with you; he'll think they look down on him while those who spend time with you do him good; so you should expect friendship, rather than enmity, to result from this affair.

"Another point: lovers generally start to desire your body before they know your character or have any experience of your other traits, with the result that even they can't tell whether they'll still want to be friends with you after their desire has passed. Non-lovers, on the other hand, are friends with you even before they achieve their goal, and you've no reason to expect that benefits received will ever detract from their friendship for you. No, those things will stand as reminders of more to come.

"Another point: you can expect to become a better person if you are won over by me, rather than by a lover. A lover will praise what you say and what you do far beyond what is best, partly because he is afraid of being disliked, and partly because desire has impaired his judgment. Here is how love draws conclusions: When a lover suffers a reverse that would cause no pain to anyone else, love makes him think he's accursed! And when he has a stroke of luck that's not worth a moment's pleasure, love compels him to sing its praises. The result is, you should feel sorry for lovers, not admire them.

"If my argument wins you over, I will, first of all, give you my time with no thought of immediate pleasure; I will plan instead for the benefits that are to come, since I am master of myself and have not been overwhelmed by love. Small problems will not make me very hostile, and big ones will make me only gradually, and only a little, angry. I will forgive you for unintentional errors and do my best to keep you from going wrong intentionally. All this, you see, is the proof of a friendship that will last a long time.

"Have you been thinking that there can be no strong friendship in the absence of erotic love? Then you ought to remember that we would not care so much about our children if that were so, or about our fathers and mothers. And we wouldn't have had any trustworthy friends, since those relationships did not come from such a desire but from doing quite different things.

"Besides, if it were true that we ought to give the biggest favor to those who need it most, then we should all be helping out the very poorest people, not the best ones, because people we've saved from the worst troubles will give us the most thanks. For instance, the right people to invite to a dinner party would be beggars and people who need to sate their hunger, because they're the ones who'll be fond of us, follow us, knock on our doors,[25] take the most pleasure with the deepest gratitude, and pray for our success. No, it's proper, I suppose, to grant your favors to those who are best able to return them, not to those in the direst need—that is, not to those who merely desire the thing, but to those who really deserve it—not to people who will take pleasure in the bloom of your youth, but to those who will share their goods with you when you are older; not to people who achieve their goal and then boast about it in public, but to those who will keep a modest silence with everyone; not to people whose devotion is short-lived, but to those who will be steady friends their whole lives; not to the people who look for an excuse to quarrel as soon as their desire has passed, but to those who will prove their worth when the bloom of your youth has faded. Now, remember what I said and keep this in mind: friends often criticize a lover for bad behavior; but no one close to a non-lover ever thinks that desire has led him into bad judgment about his interests.

"And now I suppose you'll ask me whether I'm urging you to give your favors to everyone who is not in love with you. No. As I see it, a lover would not ask you to give in to all your lovers either. You would not, in that case, earn

---

25. "Follow us, knock on our doors": classic behavior in ancient Greek literature of a lovesick man pursuing his prey.

as much gratitude from each recipient, and you would not be able to keep one affair secret from the others in the same way. But this sort of thing is not supposed to cause any harm, and really should work to the benefit of both sides.

"Well, I think this speech is long enough. If you are still longing for more, if you think I have passed over something, just ask."[26]

How does the speech strike you, Socrates? Don't you think it's simply superb, especially in its choice of words?

234D So. It's a miracle, my friend; I'm in ecstasy. And it's all your doing, Phaedrus. I was looking at you while you were reading and it seemed to me the speech had made you radiant with delight; and since I believe you understand these matters better than I do, I followed your lead, and following you I shared your Bacchic frenzy.

Ph. Come, Socrates, do you think you should joke about this?

So. Do you really think I am joking, that I am not serious?

234E Ph. You are not at all serious, Socrates. But now tell me the truth, in the name of Zeus, god of friendship: Do you think that any other Greek could say anything more impressive or more complete on this same subject?

So. What? Must we praise the speech on the ground that its author has said what the situation demanded, and not instead simply on the ground that he has spoken in a clear and concise manner, with a precise turn of phrase? If we must, I will have to go along for your sake, since—surely 235A because I am so ignorant—that passed me by. I paid attention only to the speech's style. As to the other part, I wouldn't even think that Lysias himself could be satisfied with it.[27] For it seemed to me, Phaedrus—unless, of course, you disagree—that he said the same things two or even three times,

---

26. The Greek puns on this other meaning: "If you are still longing for love, if you think I have passed over something." What the speaker has passed over and left implicit, of course, is his interest in sex.

27. Socrates' attempt to distinguish style from content at this point is probably new in the history of rhetoric, and is developed by Aristotle. See Cole, *The Origins of Rhetoric in Ancient Greece*, p. 11.

as if he really didn't have much to say about the subject, almost as if he just weren't very interested in it. In fact, he seemed to me to be showing off, trying to demonstrate that he could say the same thing in two different ways, and say it just as well both times.

PH. You are absolutely wrong, Socrates. That is in fact the best thing about the speech: He has omitted nothing worth mentioning about the subject, so that no one will ever be able to add anything of value to complete what he has already said himself. 235B

So. You go too far: I can't agree with you about that. If, as a favor to you, I accept your view, I will stand refuted by all the people—wise men and women of old—who have spoken or written about this subject.

PH. Who are these people? And where have you heard anything better than this? 235C

So. I can't tell you offhand, but I'm sure I've heard better somewhere; perhaps it was the lovely Sappho or the wise Anacreon or even some writer of prose.[28] So, what's my evidence? The fact, my dear friend, that my breast is full and I feel I can make a different speech, even better than Lysias'. Now I am well aware that none of these ideas can have come from me—I know my own ignorance.[29] The only other possibility, I think, is that I was filled, like an empty jar, by the words of other people streaming in through my ears,[30] 235D

---

28. Sappho and Anacreon were known for their poetry about love. What Socrates claims here to have learned from them is probably the idea that *erōs* is a kind of madness. See the Appendix. Socrates makes a similar appeal to authority at *Meno* 81a4, when, in order to explain how learning is possible, he introduces the idea that the soul is immortal and that knowledge is recollection. That appeal too is made to both male and female authorities.

29. For Socrates' avowal of ignorance, cf. *Apology* 24b4–5.

30. "That I was filled, like an empty jar, by the words of other people": Some scholars suspect that by using the expression "empty jar," Plato is making an allusion to Democritus (DK 68A126a) here, though others doubt that Plato, who does not once mention Democritus in his writings, would allude to him in any way. De Vries offers a full discussion of the issue.

though I'm so stupid that I've even forgotten where and from whom I heard them.

PH. But, my dear friend, you couldn't have said a better thing! Don't bother telling me when and from whom you've heard this, even if I ask you—instead, do exactly what you said: You've just promised to make another speech making more points, and better ones, without repeating a word from my book. And I promise you that, like the Nine Archons, I shall set up in return a life-sized golden statue at Delphi, not only of myself but also of you.[31]

SO. You're a real friend, Phaedrus, good as gold, to think I'm claiming that Lysias failed in absolutely every respect and that I can make a speech that is different on every point from his. I am sure that that couldn't happen even to the worst possible author. In our own case, for example, do you think that anyone could argue that one should favor the non-lover rather than the lover without praising the former for keeping his wits about him or condemning the latter for losing his—points that are essential to make—and still have something left to say? I believe we must allow these points, and concede them to the speaker. In their case, we cannot praise their novelty but only their skillful arrangement; but we can praise both the arrangement and the novelty of the nonessential points that are harder to think up.

PH. I agree with you; I think that's reasonable. This, then, is what I shall do. I will allow you to presuppose that the lover is less sane than the non-lover—and if you are able to add anything of value to complete what we already have in hand, you will stand in hammered gold beside the offering of the Cypselids in Olympia.[32]

---

31. The archons were magistrates chosen by lot in classical Athens. On taking office they swore an oath to set up a golden statue if they violated the laws. (Aristotle, *Constitution of Athens* 7.1.)
32. The Cypselids were rulers of Corinth during a period of great prosperity in the seventh century B.C. We do not know what offering Phaedrus has in mind; but an ornate chest in which Cypselus was said to have been hidden as an infant was on display at Olympia.

Socrates' Challenge to Lysias

So. Oh, Phaedrus, I was only criticizing your beloved in order to tease you—did you take me seriously? Do you think I'd really try to match the product of his wisdom with a fancier speech?

Ph. Well, as far as that goes, my friend, you've fallen into your own trap. You have no choice but to give your speech as best you can: otherwise you will force us into trading vulgar jibes the way they do in comedy. Don't make me say what you said: "Socrates, if I don't know my Socrates, I must be forgetting who I am myself," or "He wanted to speak, but he was being coy." Get it into your head that we shall not leave here until you recite what you claimed to have "in your breast." We are alone, in a deserted place, and I am younger and stronger. From all this, "take my meaning" and don't make me force you to speak when you can do so willingly.[33]

236C

236D

So. But, my dear Phaedrus, I'll be ridiculous—a mere dilettante, improvising on the same topics as a seasoned professional!

Ph. Do you understand the situation? Stop playing hard to get! I know what I can say to make you give your speech.

So. Then please don't say it!

Ph. Oh, yes, I will. And what I say will be an oath. I swear to you—by which god, I wonder? How about this very plane tree?—I swear in all truth that, if you don't make your speech right next to this tree here, I shall never, never again recite another speech for you—I shall never utter another word about speeches to you!

236E

So. My oh my, what a horrible man you are! You've really found the way to force a lover of speeches to do just as you say!

Ph. So why are you still twisting and turning like that?

So. I'll stop—now that you've taken this oath. How could I possibly give up such treats?

Ph. Speak, then.

237A

So. Do you know what I'll do?

---

33. "Take my meaning": a frequently quoted line from the poet Pindar (Snell 105), used also at *Meno* 76d.

PH. What?

SO. I'll cover my head while I'm speaking. In that way, as I'm going through the speech as fast as I can, I won't get embarrassed by having to look at you and lose the thread of my argument.

PH. Just give your speech! You can do anything else you like.

SO. Come to me, O you clear-voiced Muses, whether you are called so because of the quality of your song or from the musical people of Liguria,[34] "come, take up my burden"[35] in telling the tale that this fine fellow forces upon me so that his companion may now seem to him even more clever than he did before:

237B

There once was a boy, a youth rather,[36] and he was very beautiful, and had very many lovers. One of them was wily and had persuaded him that he was not in love, though he loved the lad no less than the others. And once in pressing his suit to him, he tried to persuade him that he ought to give his favors to a man who did not love him rather than to one who did. And this is what he said:

"If you wish to reach a good decision on any topic, my boy, there is only one way to begin: You must know what the decision is about, or else you are bound to miss your target altogether. Ordinary people cannot see that they do not know the true nature of a particular subject, so they proceed as if they did; and because they do not work out an agreement at the start of the inquiry, they wind up as

237C

---

34. "Clear-voiced Muses . . . Liguria": Socrates here suggests a far-fetched etymology for a common epithet of the Muses, *ligeiai* (the clear-voiced ones), on the basis of its resemblance to the Greek name for the Ligurians, a people who lived in what is now known as the French Riviera.

35. "Come, take up my burden": The language is poetic. If it is a quotation, its source is unknown.

36. "A youth rather": *meirakiskos*, a diminutive form of *meirakion*, which refers to a young man who is no longer a child but has not yet launched a career—just the stage (the wrong stage, as Socrates claims at *Republic* 497e–498b) when people are likely to take up the study of philosophy.

you would expect[37]—in conflict with themselves and each other. Now you and I had better not let this happen to us, since we criticize it in others. Because you and I are about to discuss whether a boy should make friends with a man who loves him rather than with one who does not, we should agree on defining what love is and what effects it has. Then we can look back and refer to that as we try to find out whether to expect benefit or harm from love. Now, as everyone plainly knows, love is some kind of desire; but we also know that even men who are not in love have a desire for what is beautiful. So how shall we distinguish between a man who is in love and one who is not? We must realize that each of us is ruled by two principles which we follow wherever they lead: one is our inborn desire for pleasures, the other is our acquired judgment that pursues what is best. Sometimes these two are in agreement; but there are times when they quarrel inside us, and then sometimes one of them gains control, sometimes the other. Now when judgment is in control and leads us by reasoning toward what is best, that sort of self-control is called 'being in your right mind';[38] but when desire takes command in us and drags us without reasoning toward pleasure, then its command is known as 'outrageousness'.[39] Now outrageousness has as many names as the forms it can take, and these are quite diverse.[40] Whichever form stands out in a particular case

237D

237E

238A

---

37. "As you would expect": literally: "as they were likely to do" (*kata to eikos*).
38. "That sort of self-control is called 'being in your right mind'": Self-control, *sôphrosunê*, is the virtue that should keep one from succumbing to temptation. The word has no exact equivalent in English and has been translated "prudence," "temperance," "soundmindedness," and "clearheadedness." In our text we use two translations, depending on context: "being in your right mind" and "self-control."
39. "Outrageousness," i.e., *hubris*, which has a range of meanings from arrogance to the sort of crimes to which arrogance gives rise. Sexual assault, in particular, was considered *hubris*.
40. "And these are quite diverse": reading *polumeles kai polueides* with most editors (literally, "multilimbed and multiformed").

238B

gives its name to the person who has it—and that is not a pretty name to be called, not worth earning at all. If it is desire for food that overpowers a person's reasoning about what is best and suppresses his other desires, it is called gluttony and it gives him the name of a glutton, while if it is desire for drink that plays the tyrant and leads the man in that direction, we all know what name we'll call him then! And now it should be clear how to describe someone appropriately in the other cases: call the man by that name—sister to these others—that derives from the sister of these desires that controls him at the time. As for the desire that has led us to say all this, it should be obvious already, but I suppose things said are always better understood than things unsaid:

238C

The unreasoning desire that overpowers a person's considered impulse to do right and is driven to take pleasure in beauty, its force reinforced by its kindred desires for beauty in human bodies—this desire, all-conquering in its forceful drive, takes its name from the word for force and is called *erōs*."[41]

There, Phaedrus my friend, don't you think, as I do, that I'm in the grip of something divine?

PH. This is certainly an unusual flow of words for you, Socrates.

238D

SO. Then be quiet and listen. There's something really divine about this place, so don't be surprised if I'm quite taken by the Nymphs' madness as I go on with the speech. I'm on the edge of speaking in dithyrambs[42] as it is.

PH. Very true!

SO. Yes, and you're the cause of it. But hear me out; the attack may yet be prevented. That, however, is up to the god; what we must do is face the boy again in the speech:

---

41. "Its force reinforced": Such rhyming is common in the style of high rhetoric (cf. Agathon's speech in the *Symposium*). "Takes its name (*erōs*) from the word for force (*rhomē*)": Such farfetched and imaginative etymologies appear also to have been common in rhetoric.

42. A dithyramb was a choral poem originally connected with the worship of Dionysus and frequently narrative in content. In classical times the dithyramb became associated with an artificial style dominated by music. For Plato's attitudes toward dithyramb, see *Gorgias* 501e and

"All right then, my brave friend,[43] now we have a definition for the subject of our decision; now we have said what it really is; so let us keep that in view as we complete our discussion. What benefit or harm is likely to come from the lover or the non-lover to the boy who gives him favors? It is surely necessary[44] that a man who is ruled by desire and is a slave to pleasure will turn his boy into whatever is most pleasing to himself. Now a sick man takes pleasure in anything that does not resist him, but sees anyone who is equal or superior to him as an enemy. That is why a lover will not willingly put up with a boyfriend who is his equal or superior, but is always working to make the boy he loves weaker and inferior to himself. Now, the ignorant man is inferior to the wise one, the coward to the brave, the ineffective speaker to the trained orator, the slow-witted to the quick. By necessity, a lover will be delighted to find all these mental defects and more, whether acquired or innate in his boy; and if he does not, he will have to supply them or else lose the pleasure of the moment. The necessary consequence is that he will be jealous and keep the boy away from the good company of anyone who would make a better man of him; and that will cause him a great deal of harm, especially if he keeps him away from what would most improve his mind—and that is, in fact, divine philosophy, from which it is necessary for a lover to keep his boy a great distance away, out of fear the boy will eventually come to look down on him. He will have to invent other ways, too, of keeping

238E

239A

239B

Hippias Major 292c8; for the tradition that Gorgias' style of rhetoric was dithyrambic, see DK 82A4.

43. "My brave friend": *o pheriste*. This epic form is rare in classical Greek and here probably signals Socrates' parody of overblown rhetoric.

44. "It is surely necessary": *ankē pou*. The second half of the speech draws consequences from the definition of love given in the first half: If a man is in love, certain points follow by logical necessity. At the same time *ankē* ("necessity") suggests a subjective necessity or compulsion: since he is not in his right mind, a lover will feel compelled to behave in certain ways. In what follows, the word *ankē* is repeated pedantically with each point. On the points, see p. xxxi, note 27.

the boy in total ignorance and so in total dependence on himself. That way the boy will give his lover the most pleasure, though the harm to himself will be severe. So it will not be of any use to your intellectual development to have as your mentor and companion a man who is in love.

"Now let's turn to your physical development. If a man is bound by necessity to chase pleasure at the expense of the good, what sort of shape will he want you to be in? How will he train you, if he is in charge? You will see that what he wants is someone who is soft, not muscular, and not trained in full sunlight but in dappled shade—someone who has never worked out like a man, never touched hard, sweaty exercise. Instead, he goes for a boy who has known only a soft unmanly style of life, who makes himself pretty with cosmetics because he has no natural color at all. There is no point in going on with this description: it is perfectly obvious what other sorts of behavior follow from this. We can take up our next topic after drawing all this to a head: the sort of body a lover wants in his boy is one that will give confidence to the enemy in a war or other great crisis while causing alarm to friends and even to his lovers. Enough of that; the point is obvious.

"Our next topic is the benefit or harm to your possessions that will come from a lover's care and company. Everyone knows the answer, especially a lover: His first wish will be for a boy who has lost his dearest, kindliest and godliest possessions—his mother and father and other close relatives. He would be happy to see the boy deprived of them, since he would expect them either to block him from the sweet pleasure of the boy's company or to criticize him severely for taking it. What is more, a lover would think any money or other wealth the boy owns would only make him harder to snare and, once snared, harder to handle. It follows by absolute necessity that wealth in a boyfriend will cause his lover to envy him, while his poverty will be a delight. Furthermore, he will wish for the boy to stay wifeless, childless, and homeless for as long as possible, since that's how long he desires to go on plucking his sweet fruit.

"There are other troubles in life, of course, but some divinity has mixed most of them with a dash of immediate pleasure. A flatterer, for example, may be an awful beast and a dreadful nuisance, but nature makes flattery rather pleasant by mixing in a little culture with its words. So it is with a mistress—for all the harm we accuse her of causing—and with many other creatures of that character, and their callings: at least they are delightful company for a day. But besides being harmful to his boyfriend, a lover is simply disgusting to spend the day with. 'Youth delights youth,' as the old proverb runs—because, I suppose, friendship grows from similarity, as boys of the same age go after the same pleasures.[45] But you can even have too much of people your own age. Besides, as they say, it is miserable for anyone to be forced into anything by necessity—and this (to say nothing of the age difference) is most true for a boy with his lover. The older man clings to the younger day and night, never willing to leave him, driven by necessity and goaded on by the sting that gives him pleasure every time he sees, hears, touches, or perceives his boy in any way at all, so that he follows him around like a servant, with pleasure. 240C

240D

"As for the boy, however, what comfort or pleasure will the lover give to him during all the time they spend together? Won't it be disgusting in the extreme to see the face of that older man who's lost his looks? And everything that goes with that face—why, it is a misery even to hear them mentioned, let alone actually handle them, as you would constantly be forced to do! To be watched and guarded suspiciously all the time, with everyone! To hear praise of yourself that is out of place and excessive! And then to be falsely accused—which is unbearable when the man is sober and not only unbearable but positively shameful when he is drunk and lays into you with a pack of wild barefaced insults! 240E

"While he is still in love he is harmful and disgusting, but after his love fades he breaks his trust with you for the future, in spite of all the promises he has made with all those oaths and entreaties which just barely kept you in a relationship that was troublesome at the time, in hope of 241A

---

45. The speaker assumes here that the lover is much older than the boy.

future benefits. So, then, by the time he should pay up, he has made a change and installed a new ruling government in himself: right-minded reason in place of the madness of love. The boy does not even realize that his lover is a different man. He insists on his reward for past favors and reminds him of what they had done and said before—as if he were still talking to the same man! The lover, however, is so ashamed that he does not dare tell the boy how much he has changed or that there is no way, now that he is in his right mind and under control again, that he can stand by

241B the promises he had sworn to uphold when he was under that old mindless regime. He is afraid that if he acted as he had before he would turn out the same and revert to his old self. So now he is a refugee, fleeing from those old promises on which he must default by necessity; he, the former lover, has to switch roles and flee, since the coin has fallen the other way,[46] while the boy must chase after him, angry and cursing. All along he has been completely unaware that he should never have given his favors to a man who was in

241C love—and who therefore had by necessity lost his mind. He should much rather have done it for a man who was not in love and had his wits about him. Otherwise it follows necessarily that he'd be giving himself to a man who is deceitful, irritable, jealous, disgusting, harmful to his property, harmful to his physical fitness, and absolutely devastating to the cultivation of his soul, which truly is, and will always be, the most valuable thing to gods and men.

"These are the points you should bear in mind, my boy. You should know that the friendship of a lover arises without

241D any good will at all. No, like food, its purpose is to sate hunger. 'Do wolves love lambs? That's how lovers befriend a boy!'"[47]

---

46. "The coin has fallen the other way": In a game like tag, Plato's contemporaries used a shell that could fall dark side or light side up. Depending on the fall of the shell, one side would chase the other. The image fits because the former lover, who used to be chasing the boy, is now being chased himself.

47. "Do wolves love (*agapōsin*) lambs? That's how lovers (*erastai*, from *erōs*) befriend (*philousin*) a boy": Note the three different verbs for love.

That's it, Phaedrus. You won't hear another word from me, and you'll have to accept this as the end of the speech.

PH. But I thought you were right in the middle—I thought you were about to speak at the same length about the non-lover, to list his good points and argue that it's better to give one's favors to him. So why are you stopping now, Socrates?

SO. Didn't you notice, my friend, that even though I am criticizing the lover, I have passed beyond lyric into epic poetry?[48] What do you suppose will happen to me if I begin to praise his opposite? Don't you realize that the Nymphs to whom you so cleverly exposed me will take complete possession of me? So I say instead, in a word, that every shortcoming for which we blamed the lover has its contrary advantage, and the non-lover possesses it. Why make a long speech of it? That's enough about them both. This way my story will meet the end it deserves, and I will cross the river and leave before you make me do something even worse.

241E

242A

PH. Not yet, Socrates, not until this heat is over. Don't you see that it is almost exactly noon, "straight-up" as they say?[49] Let's wait and discuss the speeches, and go as soon as it turns cooler.

SO. You're really superhuman when it comes to speeches, Phaedrus; you're truly amazing. I'm sure you've brought into being more of the speeches that have been given during your lifetime than anyone else, whether you composed them

242B

The line is almost in the meter of epic verse, perhaps an allusion to Homer, *Iliad* 22.262–63, or to a proverb such as "Wolves love a lamb the way lovers befriend a youth." See the note on this in de Vries.

48. The meter of the last line of the speech was epic, though it is the tradition in epic poetry to glorify a hero, and this has been an attack on love (see Rowe's note). The overheated choral poems known as dithyrambs (see note 42 on 238d3) were written in lyric meters. Monodic lyric poetry, such as that of Sappho and Anacreon, was at the other extreme from epic, and traditionally complained about the effects of love (see Appendix).

49. "Don't you see that it is almost exactly noon, *'straight-up' as they say*?": The italicized words are a rather peculiar rhetorical flourish in the original. Many modern editors have bracketed them as a later addition.

yourself or in one way or another forced others to make them; with the single exception of Simmias the Theban, you are far ahead of the rest.[50] Even as we speak, I think, you're managing to cause me to produce yet another one.

Ph. Oh, how wonderful! But what do you mean? What speech?

So. My friend, just as I was about to cross the river, the familiar divine sign came to me which, whenever it occurs, holds me back from something I am about to do.[51] I thought I heard a voice coming from this very spot, forbidding me to leave until I made atonement for some offense against the gods. In effect, you see, I am a seer, and though I am not particularly good at it, still—like people who are just barely able to read and write—I am good enough for my own purposes. I recognize my offense clearly now. In fact, the soul too, my friend, is itself a sort of seer; that's why, almost from the beginning of my speech, I was disturbed by a very uneasy feeling, as Ibycus puts it, that "for offending the gods I am honored by men."[52] But now I understand exactly what my offense has been.

Ph. Tell me, what is it?

So. Phaedrus, that speech you carried with you here—it was horrible, as horrible as the speech you made me give.

Ph. How could that be?

So. It was foolish, and close to being impious. What could be more horrible than that?

Ph. Nothing—if, of course, what you say is right.

So. Well, then? Don't you believe that Love is the son of Aphrodite? Isn't he one of the gods?[53]

---

50. Simmias, a companion of Socrates, was evidently a lover of discussion (cf. *Phaedo* 85c).
51. "The familiar divine sign": Socrates' *daimonion*. Here the *daimonion* seems to have a more positive role than it does in the *Apology* at 31cd. On the question, see Rowe's note.
52. For Ibycus, and a sample of his poetry, see the Appendix.
53. This contrasts strongly with *Symposium* 202a—204a, where Diotima denies to Socrates that Love is a god and assigns Poros and Penia (Resource and Poverty) as the parents of Love. At 242e2 "or something divine" softens the contrast with the *Symposium*. On the general argu-

Socrates' Recantation

PH. This is certainly what people say.

SO. Well, Lysias certainly doesn't and neither does your speech, which you charmed me through your potion into delivering myself. But if Love is a god or something divine—which he is—he can't be bad in any way; and yet our speeches just now spoke of him as if he were. That is their offense against Love. And they've compounded it with their utter foolishness in parading their dangerous falsehoods and preening themselves over perhaps deceiving a few silly people and coming to be admired by them. *242E*

243A

And so, my friend, I must purify myself. Now for those whose offense lies in telling false stories about matters divine, there is an ancient rite of purification—Homer did not know it, but Stesichorus did. When he lost his sight for speaking ill of Helen, he did not, like Homer, remain in the dark about the reason why. On the contrary, true follower of the Muses that he was, he understood it and immediately composed these lines:

> There's no truth to that story:
> You never sailed that lovely ship,
> You never reached the tower of Troy.[54]

243B

And as soon as he completed the poem we call the Palinode, he immediately regained his sight. Now I will prove to be wiser than Homer and Stesichorus to this small extent: I will try to offer my Palinode to Love before I am punished for

---

ment here, cf. *Republic* 377d ff., where Socrates insists that nothing bad could have been done by a god.

54. Helen was a daughter of Zeus and Leda, and though she had been worshipped as a goddess at Sparta and a few other places, she appears in Homer's *Iliad* as an all-too-human woman who was carried off from her husband by Paris in the abduction that started the Trojan War. Stesichorus was a lyric and dithyrambic poet of the early sixth century B.C. In his famous Palinode, or "taking-it-back poem," he explained away the evidence for the abduction (Fragment 192 Loeb/PMG, 11 Diehl). See *Republic* 586c. Isocrates tells the same story (*Helen* 64).

speaking ill of him—with my head bare, no longer covered in shame.

PH. No words could be sweeter to my ears, Socrates.

243C SO. You see, my dear Phaedrus, you understand how shameless the speeches were, my own as well as the one in your book. Suppose a noble and gentle man, who was (or had once been) in love with a boy of similar character, were to hear us say that lovers start serious quarrels for trivial reasons and that, jealous of their beloved, they do him harm—don't you think that man would think we had been brought up among the most vulgar of sailors, totally ignorant of love 243D among the freeborn? Wouldn't he most certainly refuse to acknowledge the flaws we attributed to Love?

PH. Most probably, Socrates.

SO. Well, that man makes me feel ashamed, and as I'm also afraid of Love himself, I want to wash out the bitterness of what we've heard with a more tasteful speech. And my advice to Lysias, too, is to write as soon as possible a speech urging one to give similar favors to a lover rather than to a non-lover.

PH. You can be sure he will. For once you have spoken in praise of the lover, I will most definitely make Lysias write a speech 243E on the same topic.

SO. I do believe you will, so long as you are who you are.

PH. Speak on, then, in full confidence.

SO. Where, then, is the boy to whom I was speaking? Let him hear this speech, too. Otherwise he may be too quick to give his favors to the non-lover.

PH. He is here, always right by your side, whenever you want him.[55]

244A SO. You'll have to understand, beautiful boy, that the previous speech was by Phaedrus, Pythocles' son, from Myrrhinous,

---

55. "He is here": We have no reason to think that Phaedrus is representing himself as being courted by Socrates. Socrates' favorite is Isocrates (279b2); and Phaedrus is crazy about Lysias, as we already know. See Rowe's note.

while the one I am about to deliver is by Stesichorus, Euphemus' son, from Himera.[56] And here is how the speech should go:

"'There's no truth to that story'—that when a lover is available you should give your favors to a man who doesn't love you instead, because he is in control of himself while the lover has lost his head.[57] That would have been fine to say if madness were bad, pure and simple; but in fact the best things we have come from madness, when it is given as a gift of the god.

"The prophetess of Delphi and the priestesses at Dodona are out of their minds when they perform that fine work of theirs for all of Greece, either for an individual person or for a whole city, but they accomplish little or nothing when they are in control of themselves. We will not mention the Sybil or the others who foretell many things by means of god-inspired prophetic trances and give sound guidance to many people—that would take too much time for a point that's obvious to everyone. But here's some evidence worth adding to our case: The people who designed our language in the old days never thought of madness as something to be ashamed of or worthy of blame; otherwise they would not have used the word 'manic' for the finest experts of all— the ones who tell the future—thereby weaving insanity into prophecy. They thought it was wonderful when it came as a gift of the god, and that's why they gave its name to prophecy; but nowadays people don't know the fine points, so they stick in a 't' and call it 'mantic.'[58] Similarly, the clear-

244B

244C

---

56. Etymologically: "Stesichorus son of Good Speaker, from the Land of Desire" (see 243a–b with note 54). Myrrhinous was one of the demes of ancient Athens.
57. See 231d. This argument was advanced in the speech of Lysias, but only half of it showed up in the earlier speech of Socrates. There Socrates broke off before arguing that a non-lover is in his right mind.
58. The words for madness (*manikē*) and prophecy (*mantikē*) are similar but not actually related. *Mantikē* refers specifically to the uttering, by inspired women, of messages from the gods that are unintelligible to ordinary human beings. Priests known as *prophētai* had the duty of

headed study of the future, which uses birds and other signs, was originally called *oionoïstic*, since it uses reasoning to bring intelligence and learning into human thought;[59] but now modern speakers call it *oiōnistic*, putting on airs with their long 'ō'. To the extent, then, that prophecy, *mantic*, is more perfect and more admirable than sign-based prediction, *oiōnistic*, in both name and achievement, madness[60] from a god is finer than self-control of human origin, according to the testimony of the ancient language givers.

"Next, madness can provide relief from the greatest plagues of trouble that beset certain families because of their guilt for ancient crimes: it turns up among those who need a way out; it gives prophecies and takes refuge in prayers to the gods and in worship, discovering mystic rites and purifications that bring the man it touches[61] through to safety for this and all time to come. So it is that the right sort of madness finds relief from present hardships for a man it has possessed.

"Third comes the kind of madness that is possession by the Muses, which takes a tender virgin soul and awakens it to a Bacchic frenzy of songs and poetry that glorifies the achievements of the past and teaches them to future generations. If anyone comes to the gates of poetry and expects to become an adequate poet by acquiring expert knowledge[62]

---

translating these utterances into ordinary Greek. On the use of farfetched etymology in rhetoric, see 238c and our note.

59. "Intelligence": *nous*; "learning": *historia*. Plato fancifully locates components of both words within the term *oionoïstic*.

60. "Madness": *mania*.

61. "The man it touches": i.e., a person who is mad (reading *heautēs* with the manuscripts).

62. Expert knowledge, *technē*, is the sort of practical knowledge that can be learned from a teacher or taught to an apprentice. Often translated "skill," "craft," or "art," *technē* can cover such practices as medicine, rhetoric, politics, and the science of war as well as such crafts as shoemaking. The Platonic Socrates frequently contrasts *technē* with inspiration; see the *Ion* (throughout), *Apology* 22bc, and *Meno* 99d. Later in the *Phaedrus*, he will investigate the possibility of a *technē* of rhetoric. In those passages, we have generally translated the word as "art,"

of the subject without the Muses' madness, he will fail, and his self-controlled verses will be eclipsed by the poetry of men who have been driven out of their minds.

"There you have some of the fine achievements—and I 245B could tell you even more—that are due to god-sent madness. We must not have any fear on this particular point, then, and we must not let anyone disturb us or frighten us with the claim that you should prefer a friend who is in control of himself to one who is disturbed. Besides proving that point, if he is to win his case, our opponent must show that love is not sent by the gods as a benefit to a lover and his boy. And we, for our part, must prove the opposite, that this sort of madness is given us by the gods to ensure our greatest good fortune. It will be a proof that convinces the 245C wise if not the clever.

"Now we must first understand the truth about the nature of the soul, divine or human, by examining what it does and what is done to it. Here begins the proof:[63]

"Every soul is immortal.[64] That is because whatever is always in motion is immortal, while what moves, and is moved by, something else stops living when it stops moving. So it is only what moves itself that never desists from motion, since it does not leave off being itself. In fact, this self-mover is also the source[65] and spring of motion in everything else that moves; and a source has no beginning. That is because anything that has a beginning comes from some source, but 245D there is no source for this, since a source that got its start

---

sometimes qualified by the adjective "systematic." See also Introduction, n. 26.

63. The argument that follows, for the immortality of the self-moving soul, is based on one given by Alcmeon of Croton, a Pythagorean of the early fifth century B.C. (Aristotle, *De Anima* 405a29 ff). See the analysis of Alcmeon's argument in Barnes, *The Presocratic Philosophers*, pp. 114–120.

64. "Every soul": The Greek allows, and some translators prefer, "all soul."

65. "Source": *archē*, often translated by the technical expression "first principle."

from something else would no longer be the source.⁶⁶ And since it cannot have a beginning, then necessarily it cannot be destroyed. That is because if a source were destroyed it could never get started again from anything else and nothing else could get started from it—that is, if everything gets started from a source. This then is why a self-mover is a source of motion. And *that* is incapable of being destroyed or starting up; otherwise all heaven and everything that has been started up⁶⁷ would collapse, come to a stop, and never have cause to start moving again. But since we have found that a self-mover is immortal, we should have no qualms about declaring that this is the very essence and principle of a soul, for every bodily object that is moved from outside has no soul, while a body whose motion comes from within, from itself, does have a soul, that being the nature of a soul; and if this is so—that whatever moves itself is essentially a soul—then it follows necessarily that soul should have neither birth nor death.

"That, then, is enough about the soul's immortality. Now here is what we must say about its structure. To describe what the soul actually is would require a very long account, altogether a task for a god in every way; but to say what it is like⁶⁸ is humanly possible and takes less time. So let us

---

66. The text here is uncertain, as the manuscript reading does not seem to make sense. We follow many editors in taking Cicero's Latin translation of the passage as evidence for the better reading. For comparison, here is Rowe's rendering of the passage as we have it from the manuscripts: "if a first principle came into being from anything, it would not do so from a first principle (*archē*)." So also de Vries.

67. "Everything that has been started up": *pasan te genesin*. Another problem with the text: here we read *genesin* with Rowe and de Vries, following the manuscripts. Burnet prints a reading derived from Philoponus, *gēn eis hen*, which would translate something like this: "otherwise all heaven and earth would collapse into one . . ." But there is no good reason not to follow the manuscripts here.

68. "What it is like": *eoiken*, a verb related to *eikos*. The idea is that it is difficult, if not impossible, to give a literal description of the soul, but that it is possible to offer a simile for it. Socrates here seems to be following literally the practice of appealing to *to eikos* which he later attributes to Tisias (273b ff.). The difference, of course, is that, unlike

do the second in our speech. Let us then liken the soul to the natural union of a team of winged horses and their charioteer. The gods have horses and charioteers that are themselves all good and come from good stock besides, while everyone else has a mixture. To begin with, our driver[69] is in charge of a pair of horses; second, one of his horses is beautiful and good and from stock of the same sort, while the other is the opposite and has the opposite sort of bloodline. This means that chariot-driving in our case is inevitably a painfully difficult business.

"And now I should try to tell you why living things are said to include both mortal and immortal beings.[70] All soul looks after all that lacks a soul, and patrols all of heaven, taking different shapes at different times. So long as its wings are in perfect condition it flies high, and the entire universe is its dominion; but a soul that sheds its wings wanders until it lights on something solid, where it settles and takes on an earthly body, which then, owing to the power of this soul, seems to move itself. The whole combination of soul and body is called a living thing, or animal, and has the designation 'mortal' as well. Such a combination cannot be immortal, not on any reasonable account. In fact it is pure fiction, based neither on observation nor on adequate reasoning, that a god is an immortal living thing which has a body and a soul, and that these are bound together by nature for all time—but of course we must let this be as it may please the gods, and speak accordingly.

Tisias, he presents an appeal to what is likely as just that, and does not claim that it is the truth (277d ff.).

69. "Our driver": *archōn* (the word used for "ruling" at 237d). The chariot driver is a potent symbol of control in ancient Greek culture. A number of related motifs in Greek art also show human figures subduing nonhuman ones. The image was used in erotic poetry for the way a lover feels when he is under the control of the one he loves. See Anacreon, Fragment 360, in the Appendix.

70. "Why living things are said to include both mortal and immortal beings": Socrates is preparing to reject the standard view of gods as immortal living things composed of body and soul, adding a cautionary note at 246d (for which cf. 229c–d).

246E

"Let us turn to what causes the shedding of the wings, what makes them fall away from a soul. It is something of this sort: By their nature wings have the power to lift up heavy things and raise them aloft where the gods all dwell, and so, more than anything that pertains to the body, they are akin to the divine, which has beauty, wisdom, goodness, and everything of that sort. These nourish the soul's wings, which grow best in their presence; but foulness and ugliness make the wings shrink and disappear.

247A

"Now Zeus, the great commander in heaven, drives his winged chariot first in the procession, looking after everything and putting all things in order. Following him is an army of gods and spirits arranged in eleven sections.[71] Hestia is the only one who remains at the home of the gods; all the rest of the twelve are lined up in formation, each god in command of the unit to which he is assigned.[72] Inside heaven

---

71. The twelve principal gods were central to civic religion in classical Greece; an altar to the Twelve placed in the marketplace of Athens (Thucydides 6.5) was considered the center of the city for purposes of measurement (Herodotus ii.7). Plato's pupil Eudoxus was probably the first to assign the Twelve to the signs of the zodiac. He listed Zeus, Hera, Poseidon, Demeter, Apollo, Artemis, Ares, Aphrodite, Hermes, Athena, Hephaestus, and Hestia. But the official representation of the Twelve in Athens showed Dionysus as twelfth instead of Hestia, and other cities used different lists.

Here, the chorus divides into eleven sections because Hestia, goddess of the hearth, stays at the home to which the chorus returns after its journey. There is always a symbolic hearth at the center of the orchestra in an ancient theater (see following note).

72. For the procession of gods to a banquet, see *Iliad* 1.423–24 and 493–95. In some ways, the gods' procession is like the apparent motion of constellations around the sky, except that the space outside heaven is visualized as a plain and not a larger sphere (248b6). In other ways, the image developed here is suggestive of the ancient Greek theater. It is as if a chorus of dancers were marshaled in military formation (as often in Greek theater), each group under the leadership of a god, moving outward from the central hearth along the aisles (*diexodoi*) among wonderful places from which to look (*makariai theai*) and around the highest tier of seats (*hapsis*) to see over the top of the theater of

are many wonderful places from which to look and many aisles which the blessed gods take up and back, each seeing to his own work, while anyone who is able and wishes to do so follows along, since jealousy has no place in the gods' chorus. When they go to feast at the banquet they have a *247B* steep climb to the high tier at the rim of heaven; on this slope the god's chariots move easily, since they are balanced and well under control, but the other chariots barely make it. The heaviness of the bad horse drags its charioteer toward the earth and weighs him down if he has failed to train it well, and this causes the most extreme toil and struggle that a soul will face. But when the souls we call immortals[73] reach the top, they move outward and take their stand on the high ridge of heaven, where its circular motion carries them *247C* around as they stand while they gaze upon what is outside heaven.

"The place beyond heaven—none of our earthly poets has ever sung or ever will sing its praises enough! Still, this is the way it is—risky as it may be, you see, I must attempt to speak the truth, especially since the truth is my subject. What is in this place is without color and without shape and without solidity, a being that really is what it is,[74] the subject of all true knowledge, visible only to intelligence, the soul's steersman. Now a god's mind is nourished by intelligence *247D* and pure knowledge, as is the mind of any soul that is

---

heaven to the plain outside and below. Appropriately, given Plato's views on theater, the image reverses the usual arrangement: the best seats in heaven are farthest from the center, and the things to see are outside the space altogether. Moreover, this cannot physically be a theater, since movement within the space of heaven is by winged flight.
73. "The souls we call immortals": the gods. All souls are immortal, on Plato's theory, but "immortals" was a common way of referring to the gods.
74. "That really is what it is": *ousia ontōs ousa*. A way of referring to the supreme entities in Plato's theory of reality, the transcendent Forms such as Justice and Beauty. In this paragraph, Socrates has temporarily abandoned the imagery of the procession of winged souls and speaks directly about Reality in the technical language of philosophy; for the risk see 246a.

concerned to take in what is appropriate to it, and so it is delighted at last to be seeing what is real and watching what is true, feeding on all this and feeling wonderful, until the circular motion brings it around to where it started. On the way around it has a view of Justice as it is; it has a view of Self-control; it has a view of Knowledge—not the knowledge that is close to change, that becomes different as it knows the different things which we consider real down here.[75] No, it is the knowledge of what really is what it is. And when the soul has seen all the things that are as they are and feasted on them, it sinks back inside heaven and goes home. On its arrival, the charioteer stables the horses by the manger, throws in ambrosia, and gives them nectar to drink besides.[76]

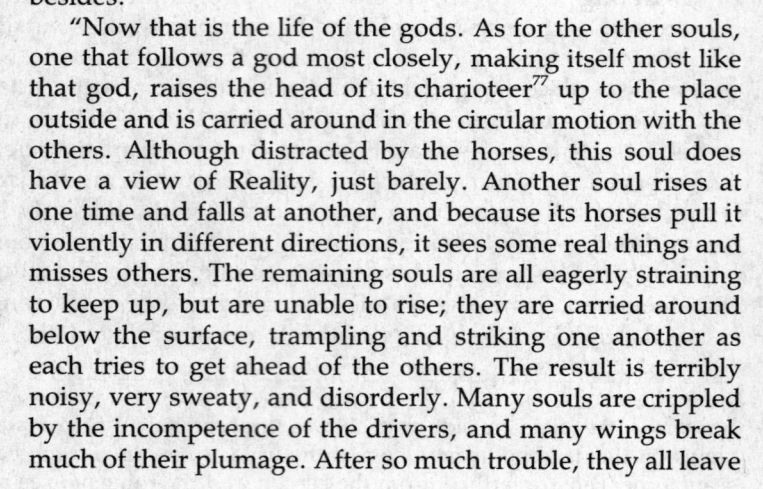

"Now that is the life of the gods. As for the other souls, one that follows a god most closely, making itself most like that god, raises the head of its charioteer[77] up to the place outside and is carried around in the circular motion with the others. Although distracted by the horses, this soul does have a view of Reality, just barely. Another soul rises at one time and falls at another, and because its horses pull it violently in different directions, it sees some real things and misses others. The remaining souls are all eagerly straining to keep up, but are unable to rise; they are carried around below the surface, trampling and striking one another as each tries to get ahead of the others. The result is terribly noisy, very sweaty, and disorderly. Many souls are crippled by the incompetence of the drivers, and many wings break much of their plumage. After so much trouble, they all leave

---

75. What is it for knowledge to "become different"? The idea may be that, in contrast to the single, unified knowledge of the whole real world which Plato considers the only knowledge worth the name, knowledge of sensible objects is fragmented; for example, knowledge of the stars and their properties is astronomy, knowledge of numbers and their properties is arithmetic, and so on.
76. See *Iliad* 5.368 ff.
77. See 247c7: The objects outside are visible only to the charioteer ("the soul's steersman").

without having seen reality, uninitiated, and when they have gone they will depend on what they think is nourishment—their own opinions.

"The reason there is so much eagerness to see the plain where truth stands is that this pasture has the grass that is the right food for the best part of the soul, and it is the nature of the wings that lift up the soul to be nourished by it. Besides, the law of Destiny is this:[78] If any soul becomes a companion to a god and catches sight of any true thing, it will be unharmed until the next circuit; and if it is able to do this every time, it will always be safe.[79] If, on the other hand, it does not see anything true because it could not keep up, and by some accident takes on a burden of forgetfulness and wrongdoing, then it is weighed down, sheds its wings and falls to earth. At that point, according to the law, the soul is not born into a wild animal in its first incarnation; but a soul that has seen the most will be planted in the seed of a man who will become a lover of wisdom[80] or of beauty, or[81] who will be cultivated in the arts and prone to erotic love. The second sort of soul will be put into someone who will be a lawful king or warlike commander; the third, a statesman, a manager of a household, or a financier; the fourth will be a trainer who loves exercise or a doctor who cures the body; the fifth will lead the life of a prophet[82] or priest of the mysteries. To the sixth the life of a poet or some other representational artist is properly assigned; to the seventh the life of a manual laborer or farmer; to the

---

78. "The law of Destiny": *Adrasteia* (Destiny) is a personification of necessity, who governs human conduct and is especially given to punishing people who make arrogant claims (cf. *Republic* 451a3).

79. "Safe": i.e., not forced to enter a body.

80. "Lover of wisdom": i.e., a philosopher.

81. The disjunctions between philosophers, lovers of beauty, and cultivated men are *exclusive*, so that the first group includes three different categories (cf. the fourth, whose members are trainers or doctors, but not both).

82. "The life of a prophet": *mantikos bios*. A *mantis* is one who speaks a god's words directly.

eighth the career of a sophist or demagogue, and to the ninth a tyrant.[83]

"Of all these, any who have led their lives with justice will change to a better fate, and any who have led theirs with injustice, to a worse one. In fact, no soul returns to the place from which it came for ten thousand years, since its wings will not grow before then, except for the soul of a man who practices philosophy without guile or who loves boys philosophically. If, after the third cycle of one thousand years, the last-mentioned souls have chosen such a life three times in a row, they grow their wings back, and they depart in the three-thousandth year. As for the rest, once their first life is over, they come to judgment; and, once judged, some are condemned to go to places of punishment beneath the earth and pay the full penalty for their injustice, while the others are lifted up by justice to a place in heaven where they live in the manner the life they led in human form has earned them. In the thousandth year both groups arrive at a choice and allotment of second lives, and each soul chooses the life it wants.[84] From there, a human soul can enter a wild animal, and a soul that was once human can move from an animal to a human being again. But a soul that never saw the truth cannot take a human shape, since a human being must understand speech in terms of general forms, proceeding to bring many perceptions together into a reasoned unity.[85] That process is the recollection of the things our soul

---

83. A *sophist* is a paid teacher. A *demagogue* is a politician who does not hold public office but exerts influence on the people through the use of rhetoric. A *tyrant* is a sole ruler who is not a traditional monarch but depends on the force of armed men to stay in power (*Republic* 565e–566c).
84. "Each soul chooses the life it wants": At 248e each soul's fate was determined by its merits. Here choice plays a role. See *Republic* 617e ff., and contrast this with *Timaeus* 42b ff., which rules out the element of choice altogether.
85. The Greek text is difficult to interpret here. We accept Badham's emendation of *iont'* for *ion*.

saw when it was traveling with god, when it disregarded the things we now call real and lifted up its head to what is truly real instead.[86]

"For just this reason it is fair that only a philosopher's mind grows wings,[87] since its memory always keeps it as close as possible to those realities by being close to which the gods are divine. A man who uses reminders of these things[88] correctly is always at the highest, most perfect level of initiation, and he is the only one who is perfect as perfect can be. He stands outside human concerns and draws close to the divine; ordinary people think he is disturbed and rebuke him for this, unaware that he is possessed by god.[89] Now this takes me to the whole point of my discussion of the fourth kind of madness—that which someone shows when he sees the beauty we have down here and is reminded of true beauty; then he takes wing and flutters in his eagerness to rise up, but is unable to do so; and he gazes aloft, like a bird, paying no attention to what is down below— and that is what brings on him the charge that he has gone mad. This is the best and noblest of all the forms that possession by god can take for anyone who has it or is connected to it, and when someone who loves beautiful boys is touched

249D

249E

---

86. For the theory of Recollection see also *Meno* 80d ff. and (what is closer in doctrine to the *Phaedrus*) *Phaedo* 72e ff. According to the *Phaedo*, Recollection explains how I know a general concept (such as Equality) under which I classify many perceptions (such as these sticks that I see to be of equal length). Since I have never perceived Equality, but am aware of the concept each time I see that two sticks are equal, I must be recollecting the concept each time I use it.
87. "Only a philosopher's mind grows wings": that is, before ten thousand years are up.
88. "Reminders of these things": The reference is to things we perceive on earth, such as a boy's beauty, that should remind a philosopher of heavenly Beauty.
89. "Possessed by god": *enthousiazōn*. The term, which also occurs at 241e, 253a, 263d, and a few lines below in the present discussion, suggests both ecstasy, being beside oneself, and the presence of a god (*theos*) within (*en*) a person.

by this madness he is called a lover.[90] As I said,[91] nature requires that the soul of every human being has seen reality; otherwise, no soul could have entered this sort of living thing.[92] But not every soul is easily reminded of the reality there by what it finds here—not souls that got only a brief glance at the reality there, not souls who had such bad luck when they fell down here that they were twisted by bad company into lives of injustice so that they forgot the sacred objects they had seen before. Only a few remain whose memory is good enough; and they are startled when they see an image of what they saw up there. Then they are beside themselves, and their experience is beyond their comprehension because they cannot fully grasp what it is that they are seeing.

"Justice and self-control do not shine out through their images down here, and neither do the other objects of the soul's admiration; the senses are so murky that only a few people are able to make out, with difficulty, the original of the likenesses they encounter here. But beauty was radiant to see at that time when the souls, along with the glorious chorus (we[93] were with Zeus, while others followed other gods), saw that blessed and spectacular vision and were ushered into the mystery that we may rightly call the most blessed of all. And we who celebrated it were wholly perfect and free of all the troubles that awaited us in time to come, and we gazed in rapture at sacred revealed objects that were perfect, and simple, and unshakeable and blissful.[94] That

---

90. Cf. 248d3 for the ranking. Socrates may mean to derive *erastēs* ("lover") from *erōs* ("love") and *aristos* ("best").
91. "As I said": at 249b5–6.
92. "This sort of living thing": a human being.
93. "We": we philosophers; cf. 252e. This confident claim, so uncharacteristic of Socrates in general and of his portrait in the *Phaedrus* in particular, should make us pause before attributing directly to him (or, for that matter, to Plato) the views he is made to express in the speech. As we argued in the Introduction, Socrates, as a "true" rhetorician, may be projecting an image he judges Phaedrus will find attractive.
94. "We gazed in rapture at sacred revealed objects that were perfect, and simple, and unshakeable and blissful": This is the language of

was the ultimate vision, and we saw it in pure light because we were pure ourselves, not buried in this thing we are carrying around now, which we call a body, locked in it like an oyster in its shell.

"Well, all that was for love of a memory that made me stretch out my speech in longing for the past. Now beauty, as I said, was radiant among the other objects; and now that we have come down here we grasp it sparkling through the clearest of our senses. Vision, of course, is the sharpest of our bodily senses, although it does not see wisdom. It would awaken a terribly powerful love if an image of wisdom came through our sight as clearly as beauty does, and the same goes for the other objects of inspired love. But now beauty alone has this privilege, to be the most clearly visible and the most loved. Of course a man who was initiated long ago or who has become defiled is not to be moved abruptly from here to a vision of Beauty itself when he sees what we call beauty here;[95] so instead of gazing at the latter reverently, he surrenders to pleasure and sets out in the manner of a four-footed beast, eager to make babies; and, wallowing in vice, he goes after unnatural pleasure too, without a trace of fear or shame.[96] A recent initiate, however, one who has seen much in heaven—when he sees a godlike face or bodily form that has captured Beauty well, first he shudders and a fear comes over him like those he felt at the earlier time; then he gazes at him with the reverence due a god, and if he weren't afraid people would think him completely mad,

250D

250E

251A

---

initiation into the highest level of a mystery religion, the *epopteia*, or stage at which the initiate is given a view of the sacred objects of the cult—an experience which is supposed to change his life. As the adjectives at the end of the sentence indicate, the revealed objects (*phasmata*) in this special case are not religious symbols but the Forms themselves (cf. the allusion to initiation at 249c).

95. "What we call beauty": literally, "what is named after it." In Plato's theory, an earthly beauty is called that only because it is a likeness of the heavenly Beauty.

96. For Plato's attitude toward homosexual acts, see *Laws* 636c, 835d–842a.

251B he'd even sacrifice to his boy as if he were the image of a god. Once he has looked at him, his chill gives way to sweating and a high fever,[97] because the stream of beauty that pours into him through his eyes[98] warms him up and waters the growth of his wings. Meanwhile, the heat warms him and melts the places where the wings once grew, places that were long ago closed off with hard scabs to keep the sprouts from coming back; but as nourishment flows in, the feather shafts swell and rush to grow from their roots beneath every part of the soul (long ago, you see, the entire soul had wings).
251C Now the whole soul seethes and throbs in this condition. Like a child whose teeth are just starting to grow in, and its gums are all aching and itching—that is exactly how the soul feels when it begins to grow wings. It swells up and aches and tingles as it grows them. But when it looks upon the beauty of the boy and takes in the stream of particles flowing into it from his beauty (that is why this is called 'desire'[99]), when it is watered and warmed by this, then all its pain
251D subsides and is replaced by joy. When, however, it is separated from the boy and runs dry, then the openings of the passages in which the feathers grow are dried shut and keep the wings from sprouting. Then the stump of each feather is blocked in its desire and it throbs like a pulsing artery while the feather pricks at its passageway, with the result that the whole soul is stung all around, and the pain simply drives it wild—but then, when it remembers the boy in his beauty, it recovers its joy. From the outlandish mix of these

---

97. Plato's account of the reaction of a philosophical lover to the sight of a beautiful boy probably owes a debt to Sappho. See 235c and the poems translated in the Appendix.
98. "The stream of beauty that pours into him through his eyes": The idea that perception is due to particles (cf. 251c) flowing from the perceived object through a sense organ is suggestive of a theory attributed to Empedocles (*Meno* 76c–d) and developed by Plato in the *Timaeus* (45b–c and 67d–e).
99. "Desire": *himeros*: The derivation is from *merē* ("particles"), *ienai* ("go") and *rhein* ("flow"). For a different but equally fanciful Platonic derivation of the same word, see *Cratylus* 420a.

two feelings—pain and joy—comes anguish and helpless raving: in its madness the lover's soul cannot sleep at night 251E or stay put by day; it rushes, yearning, wherever it expects to see the person who has that beauty. When it does see him, it opens the sluice-gates of desire and sets free the parts that were blocked up before. And now that the pain and the goading have stopped, it can catch its breath and once more suck in, for the moment, this sweetest of all pleasures. This it is not at all willing to give up, and no one is more 252A important to it than the beautiful boy. It forgets mother and brothers and friends entirely and doesn't care at all if it loses its wealth through neglect. And as for proper and decorous behavior, in which it used to take pride, the soul despises the whole business. Why, it is even willing to sleep like a slave,[100] anywhere, as near to the object of its longing as it is allowed to get! That is because in addition to its reverence for one who has such beauty, the soul has discovered that 252B the boy is the only doctor for all that terrible pain.

"This is the experience we humans call love, you beautiful boy (I mean the one to whom I am making this speech).[101] You are so young that what the gods call it is likely to strike you as funny. Some of the successors of Homer, I believe, report two lines from the less well known poems, of which the second is quite indecent and does not scan very well. They praise love this way:

> Yes, mortals call him powerful winged 'Love';
> But because of his need to thrust out the wings,
>   the gods call him 'Shove.'[102]

---

100. "To sleep like a slave": Stereotypical lovers slept at the gates of their loved ones; slaves had their cubicles near the gate of a house.
101. "The one to whom I am making this speech": not Phaedrus, who is not a boy, but the boy who was courted by the "non-lover" in the fictional example.
102. The lines are probably Plato's invention, as the language is not consistently Homeric. The pun in the original is on *erōs* and *pterōs* ("the winged one"). The error in meter is the treatment of *de* as short before two consonants. The indecency is in the word *pterophutōr* ("wing-thrusting"). John Cooper helped with the English version presented here.

252C You may believe this or not as you like. But, seriously, the cause of love is as I have said, and this is how lovers really feel.

"If the man who is taken by love used to be an attendant on Zeus, he will be able to bear the burden of this feathered force with dignity.[103] But if it is one of Ares'[104] troops who has fallen prisoner of love—if that is the god with whom he took the circuit—then if he has the slightest suspicion that the boy he loves has done him wrong, he turns murderous, and he is ready to make a sacrifice of himself as well as the boy.

252D "So it is with each of the gods: everyone spends his life honoring the god in whose chorus he danced, and emulates that god in every way he can, so long as he remains undefiled and in his first life down here. And that is how he behaves with everyone at every turn, not just with those he loves. Everyone chooses his love after his own fashion from among those who are beautiful, and then treats the boy like his very
252E own god, building him up and adorning him as an image to honor and worship. Those who followed Zeus, for example, choose someone to love who is a Zeus himself in the nobility of his soul.[105] So they make sure he has a talent for philosophy and the guidance of others, and once they have found him and are in love with him they do everything to develop that talent. If any lovers have not yet embarked on this practice,[106] then they start to learn, using any source they can and also making progress on their own. They are well equipped to track down their god's true nature with their own resources
253A because of their driving need to gaze at the god,[107] and as

---

103. Those who followed Zeus turn out to be philosophers. Cf. 246e6, 250b7.
104. Ares is the god of war.
105. The Greek here puns gently on the genitive of Zeus's name (*Dios*) and the adjective "noble" (*dios*). Zeus, the father of gods and of men, wielder of lightning bolts, has the highest dignity of the gods and a special affinity with kings. He is often seen as the defender of justice.
106. "Not yet embarked on this practice": i.e., haven't yet learned how to develop a boy's talent—in this case for philosophy.
107. "To gaze at the god": by looking at the boy who is the god's image.

they are in touch with the god by memory they are inspired by him and adopt his customs and practices, so far as a human being can share a god's life. For all of this they know they have the boy to thank, and so they love him all the more; and if they draw their inspiration from Zeus, then, like the Bacchants,[108] they pour it into the soul of the one they love in order to help him take on as much of their own god's qualities as possible. Hera's followers look for a kingly character, and once they have found him they do all the same things for him. And so it is for followers of Apollo or any other god:[109] They take their god's path and seek for their own a boy whose nature is like the god's; and when they have got him they emulate the god, convincing the boy they love and training him to follow their god's pattern and way of life, so far as is possible in each case. They show no envy, no mean-spirited lack of generosity, toward the boy, but make every possible effort to draw him into being totally like themselves and the god to whom they are devoted. This, then, is any true lover's heart's desire: if he follows that desire in the manner I described, this friend who has been driven mad by love will secure a consummation[110] for the one he has befriended that is as beautiful and blissful as I said—if, of course, he captures him. Here, then, is how the captive is caught:

"Remember how we divided each soul in three at the beginning of our story—two parts in the form of horses and

253B

253C

253D

---

108. "Like the Bacchants": Bacchants were worshippers of Dionysus (not Zeus) who gained miraculous abilities when possessed by the madness of their god (*Ion* 534a). They readily passed their inspired enthusiasm from one to another. See also Euripides' *Bacchae* 704–11.
109. Hera, associated with the earth, is the wife of Zeus and the guardian of marriage; Apollo is god of music, prophecy, healing, and the sun.
110. "Consummation": We follow Rowe and most manuscripts in reading *teleutē*, but most editors prefer *teletē*, "initiation." The meaning is essentially the same; the consummation of the affair comes when the lover shares his madness with the one he loves. For an ironic parallel, see 234d above.

the third in that of a charioteer? Let us continue with that. One of the horses, we said, is good, the other not; but we did not go into the details of the goodness of the good horse or the badness of the bad. Let us do that now. The horse that is on the right, or nobler, side is upright in frame and well jointed, with a high neck and a regal nose; his coat is white, his eyes are black, and he is a lover of honor with modesty and self-control; companion to true glory, he needs no whip, and is guided by verbal commands alone. The other horse is a crooked great jumble of limbs with a short bull-neck, a pug nose, black skin, and bloodshot white eyes; companion to wild boasts and indecency, he is shaggy around the ears—deaf as a post—and just barely yields to horsewhip and goad combined. Now when the charioteer looks in the eye of love, his entire soul is suffused with a sense of warmth and starts to fill with tingles and the goading of desire. As for the horses, the one who is obedient to the charioteer is still controlled, then as always, by its sense of shame, and so prevents itself from jumping on the boy. The other one, however, no longer responds to the whip or the goad of the charioteer; it leaps violently forward and does everything to aggravate its yokemate and its charioteer, trying to make them go up to the boy and suggest to him the pleasures of sex. At first the other two resist, angry in their belief that they are being made to do things that are dreadfully wrong. At last, however, when they see no end to their trouble, they are led forward, reluctantly agreeing to do as they have been told. So they are close to him now, and they are struck by the boy's face as if by a bolt of lightning. When the charioteer sees that face, his memory is carried back to the real nature of Beauty, and he sees it again where it stands on the sacred pedestal next to Self-control. At the sight he is frightened, falls over backwards awestruck, and at the same time has to pull the reins back so fiercely that both horses are set on their haunches, one falling back voluntarily with no resistance, but the other insolent and quite unwilling. They pull back a little further; and while one horse drenches the whole soul with sweat out of shame and awe, the other—once it has recovered from the pain caused by the bit and its fall—bursts into a torrent of insults as soon as it has caught its breath, accusing its charioteer and yokemate of all sorts of cowardice and unmanliness for abandoning their position and their agreement. Now once more it tries to make its unwilling partners advance, and gives in grudgingly only when they beg it to wait till later. Then, when the promised time arrives, and they are pretending to have forgotten, it reminds them; it struggles, it neighs, it pulls them forward and forces them to approach the boy again with the same proposition; and as soon as they are near, it drops its head, straightens its tail, bites the bit, and pulls without any shame at all. The charioteer is now struck with the same feelings as before, only worse, and he's falling back as he would from a starting gate;[111] and he violently yanks the bit back out of the teeth of the insolent horse, only harder this time, so that he bloodies its foul-speaking tongue and jaws, sets its legs and haunches firmly on the ground, and 'gives it over to pain.'[112] When the bad horse has suffered this same thing time after time, it stops being so insolent; now it is humble enough to follow the charioteer's warnings, and when it sees the beautiful boy it dies of fright, with the result that now at last the lover's soul follows its boy in reverence and awe.

"And because he is served with all the attentions due a god by a lover who is not pretending otherwise[113] but is truly in the throes of love, and because he is by nature disposed to be a friend of the man who is serving him (even if he has already been set against love by schoolfriends or others who say that it is shameful to associate with a lover, and initially rejects the lover in consequence), as time goes forward he is brought by his ripening age and a sense of what must be

---

111. "Starting gate": *husplēx*. This is the most likely meaning of the word. It probably consisted of a rope across the starting line, which would pose great danger to horses that were champing at the bit to cross the gate before the proper time.
112. "Gives it over to pain": a Homeric expression; cf. *Iliad* 5.397 and *Odyssey* 17.567.
113. "Not pretending otherwise": The speaker in Socrates' first speech was a lover pretending not to love.

to a point where he lets the man spend time with him. It is a decree of fate, you see, that bad is never friends with bad, while good cannot fail to be friends with good. Now that he allows his lover to talk and spend time with him, and the man's good will is close at hand, the boy is amazed by it as he realizes that all the friendship he has from his other friends and relatives put together is nothing compared to that of this friend who is inspired by a god.

"After the lover has spent some time doing this, staying near the boy (and even touching him during sports and on other occasions), then the spring that feeds the stream Zeus named 'Desire'[114] when he was in love with Ganymede begins to flow mightily in the lover and is partly absorbed by him, and when he is filled it overflows and runs away outside him. Think how a breeze or an echo bounces back from a smooth solid object to its source; that is how the stream of beauty goes back to the beautiful boy and sets him aflutter. It enters through his eyes, which are its natural route to the soul; there it waters the passages for the wings, starts the wings growing, and fills the soul of the loved one with love in return. Then the boy is in love, but has no idea what he loves.[115] He does not understand, and cannot explain, what has happened to him. It is as if he had caught an eye disease from someone else, but could not identify the cause;[116] he does not realize that he is seeing himself in the lover as in a mirror. So when the lover is near, the boy's pain is relieved just as the lover's is, and when they are apart he yearns as much as he is yearned for, because he has a mirror image of love in him—'backlove'—though he neither speaks nor thinks of it as love, but as friendship. Still, his desire is nearly

---

114. See the etymology for *himeros* proposed in n. 99.

115. In the classical pattern, the one who is loved does not love in return. After all, he is the only beautiful one in the picture. Hence Plato's coinage of the word "backlove" to refer to the emotion that is returned by the loved one (255e1). By contrast, friendship (*philia*) is supposed to be reciprocated.

116. The ancient Greeks thought you could catch an eye disease merely by making eye contact with an infected person.

the same as the lover's, though weaker: he wants to see, touch, kiss, and lie down with him; and of course, as you might expect, he acts on these desires soon after they occur.

"When they are in bed, the lover's undisciplined horse has a word to say to the charioteer—that after all its sufferings it is entitled to a little fun. Meanwhile, the boy's bad horse has nothing to say, but swelling with desire, confused, it hugs the lover and kisses him in delight at his great good will. And whenever they are lying together it is completely unable, for its own part, to deny the lover any favor he might beg to have. Its yokemate, however, along with its charioteer, resists such requests with modesty and reason. Now if the victory goes to the better elements in both their minds, which lead them to follow the assigned regimen of philosophy, their life here below is one of bliss and shared understanding. They are modest and fully in control of themselves now that they have enslaved the part that brought trouble into the soul and set free the part that gave it virtue. After death, when they have grown wings and become weightless, they have won the first of three rounds in these, the true Olympic Contests. There is no greater good than this that either human self-control or divine madness can offer a man. If, on the other hand, they adopt a lower way of living, with ambition in place of philosophy,[117] then pretty soon when they are careless because they have been drinking or for some other reason, the pair's undisciplined horses will catch their souls off guard and together bring them to commit that act which ordinary people would take to be the happiest choice of all; and when they have consummated it once, they go on doing this for the rest of their lives, but sparingly, since they have not approved of what they are doing with their whole minds. So these two also live in mutual friendship (though weaker than that of the philosophical pair), both while they are in love and after they have passed beyond it, because they realize they have exchanged

---

117. Ambition, the love of *timē*, is the first step down from philosophy, as described in *Republic* 549a ff. *Timē* is public recognition or public office.

such firm vows that it would be forbidden for them ever to break them and become enemies. In death they are wingless when they leave the body, but their wings are bursting to sprout, so the prize they have won from the madness of love is considerable, because those who have begun the sacred journey in lower heaven may not by law be sent into darkness for the journey under the earth; their lives are bright and happy as they travel together, and thanks to their love they will grow wings together when the time comes.

"These are the rewards you will have from a lover's friendship, my boy, and they are as great as divine gifts should be. A non-lover's companionship, on the other hand, is diluted by human self-control; all it pays are cheap, human dividends, and though the slavish attitude it engenders in a friend's soul is widely praised as virtue, it tosses the soul around for nine thousand years on the earth and leads it, mindless, beneath it.[118]

"So now, dear Love, this is the best and most beautiful palinode[119] we could offer as payment for our debt, especially in view of the rather poetical choice of words Phaedrus made me use.[120] Forgive us our earlier speeches in return for this one; be kind and gracious toward my expertise at love, which is your own gift to me:[121] do not, out of anger, take it away or disable it; and grant that I may be held in higher esteem than ever by those who are beautiful. If Phaedrus and I said anything that shocked you in our earlier speech, blame it on Lysias, who was its father, and put a stop to his making speeches of this sort; convert him to philosophy like his

---

118. "On the earth and beneath it": See *Phaedo* 81c–e.
119. "Palinode": See note 54 above.
120. Socrates has adopted a grand style to suit his hearer. The expression "in view of the . . . choice of words" repeats Phaedrus' language at 234c7. As at 238c, Socrates ironically tries to disclaim responsibility for his rhetoric.
121. "My expertise at love, which is your own gift to me": For Socrates' claim to have mastered the *technē* of love, cf. *Symposium* 177d, 212b; *Lysis* 204b.

brother Polemarchus[122] so that his lover here[123] may no longer play both sides as he does now, but simply devote his life to Love through philosophical discussions."

Ph. I join you in your prayer, Socrates. If this is really best for us, may it come to pass. As to your speech, I admired it from the moment you began: You managed it much better than your first one. I'm afraid that Lysias' effort to match it is bound to fall flat, if of course he even dares to try to offer a speech of his own. In fact, my marvelous friend, a politician I know was only recently taking Lysias to task for just that reason: All through his invective, he kept calling him a "speech writer." So perhaps his pride will keep him from writing this speech for us.

So. Ah, what a foolish thing to say, young man. How wrong you are about your friend: he can't be intimidated so easily! But perhaps you thought the man who was taking him to task meant what he said as a reproach?

Ph. He certainly seemed to, Socrates. In any case, you are surely aware yourself that the most powerful and renowned politicians are ashamed to compose speeches or leave any writings behind; they are afraid that in later times they may come to be known as "sophists."

So. Phaedrus, you don't understand the expression "Pleasant Bend"—it originally referred to the long bend of the Nile.[124] And, besides the bend, you also don't understand that the most ambitious politicians love speechwriting and long for

257C

257D

257E

---

122. On Polemarchus, see note 1 above.
123. "His lover here": Phaedrus admires Lysias (236b5, 279b3).
124. "Pleasant Bend": *glukus agkōn*. The expression has puzzled readers since ancient times. Apparently it was a familiar example of something named by language that means the opposite—though called "pleasant" it was really a long, nasty bend. Some scholars, however, take it as a term of endearment for Phaedrus, referring to an elbow's bend.

"It originally referred to the long bend of the Nile": Scholars who adopt the endearment theory treat these words as a gloss added by an ancient reader trying, wrongly, to make sense of the passage. We disagree: There is no reason to reject the clause.

their writings to survive. In fact, when they write one of their speeches, they are so pleased when people praise it that they add at the beginning a list of its admirers everywhere.

PH. What do you mean? I don't understand.

258A SO. Don't you know that the first thing politicians put in their writings[125] is the names of their admirers?

PH. How so?

SO. "Resolved," the author often begins, "by the Council" or "by the People" or by both, and "So-and-so said"[126]—meaning himself, the writer, with great solemnity and self-importance. Only then does he go on with what he has to say, showing off his wisdom to his admirers, often composing a very long document. Do you think there's any difference between that and a written speech?

258B PH. No, I don't.

SO. Well, then, if it remains on the books, he is delighted and leaves the stage a poet. But if it is struck down, if he fails as a speech writer and isn't considered worthy of having his work written down, he goes into deep mourning, and his friends along with him.

PH. He certainly does.

SO. Clearly, then, they don't feel contempt for speechwriting; on the contrary, they are in awe of it.

PH. Quite so.

258C SO. There's this too. What of an orator or a king who acquires enough power to match Lycurgus, Solon, or Darius as a lawgiver[127] and acquires immortal fame as a speech writer

---

125. The manuscript reading, *suggramati*, is impossible. We follow most recent editors in reading *suggramatos*.

126. "'Resolved,' the author often begins": This is the standard form for decisions, including legislation, made by the assembly of Athens. It is not the standard beginning for even the most political of speeches. With Phaedrus' agreement, Socrates is overlooking the difference between writing a speech and writing formal legislation.

127. Lycurgus was the legendary lawgiver of Sparta. Solon reformed the constitution of Athens in the early sixth century B.C. and was revered by both democrats and their opponents. The two were the most famous lawgivers of Greece (*Symposium* 209d). Darius, king of Persia (521–486

in his city? Doesn't he think that he is equal to the gods while he is still alive? And don't those who live in later times believe just the same about him when they behold his writings?

PH. Very much so.

So. Do you really believe then that any one of these people, whoever he is and however much he hates Lysias, would reproach him for being a writer?

PH. It certainly isn't likely in view of what you said, for he would probably be reproaching his own ambition as well.[128]

So. This, then, is quite clear: Writing speeches is not in itself a shameful thing. 258D

PH. How could it be?

So. It's not speaking or writing well that's shameful; what's really shameful is to engage in either of them shamefully or badly.

PH. That is clear.

So. So what distinguishes good from bad writing? Do we need to ask this question of Lysias or anyone else who ever did or will write anything—whether a public or a private document, poetic verse or plain prose?

PH. You ask if we need to? Why else should one live, I say, if not for pleasures of this sort? Certainly not for those you cannot feel unless you are first in pain, like most of the pleasures of the body, and which for this reason we call the pleasures of slaves.[129] 258E

B.C.), is elsewhere represented by Plato as an ideal lawgiver (*Laws* 695c–d, *Epistle* 7, 332a–b). But none of these—not even Solon—was famous as a speech writer. As at 258a, Plato is running together "speechwriting" with "writing legislation."

128. "It certainly isn't likely": The argument is an appeal to *eikos* ("what is likely"). In the absence of evidence, we don't know what these particular legislators thought of speech writers, though we do know that some legislators looked down on speechwriting. For Socrates' own attitude toward the appeal to *eikos* in argument, see 272e ff.

129. "Certainly not for those you cannot feel . . . pleasures of slaves": This sentence is probably a clumsy insertion by an ancient editor or copyist. It is pedantic and uncharacteristic of Plato, and besides is not

So. It seems we clearly have the time. Besides, I think that the cicadas, who are singing and carrying on conversations with one another in the heat of the day above our heads, are also watching us. And if they saw the two of us avoiding conversation at midday like most people, diverted by their song and, sluggish of mind, nodding off, they would have every right to laugh at us, convinced that a pair of slaves had come to their resting place to sleep like sheep gathering around the spring in the afternoon. But if they see us in conversation, steadfastly navigating around them as if they were the Sirens,[130] they will be very pleased and immediately give us the gift from the gods they are able to give to mortals.

Ph. What is this gift? I don't think I have heard of it.

So. Everyone who loves the Muses should have heard of this. The story goes that the cicadas used to be human beings who lived before the birth of the Muses. When the Muses were born and song was created for the first time, some of the people of that time were so overwhelmed with the pleasure of singing that they forgot to eat or drink; so they died without even realizing it. It is from them that the race of the cicadas came into being; and, as a gift from the Muses, they have no need of nourishment once they are born. Instead, they immediately burst into song, without food or drink, until it is time for them to die. After they die, they go to the Muses and tell each one of them which mortals have honored her. To Terpsichore they report those who have honored

---

developed in the passage that follows. The argument for authenticity is based on the occurrence of "slaves" at 259a, which may echo the "of slaves" in the questionable sentence. Our view, however, is that it is precisely because of the unexpected use of "slaves" that the editor or copyist felt the need to insert the sentence. A third alternative is that the sentence does not belong to Phaedrus but forms the beginning of Socrates' reply; but the conversation makes better sense without the sentence in either position.

130. The Sirens were birdlike women who lured sailors to shipwreck on rocky shores with their irresistible singing. Odysseus saved himself by blocking the ears of his crew and having himself tied to his mast (*Odyssey* 12).

Discussion of Rhetoric

her by their devotion to the dance and thus make them dearer to her. To Erato, they report those who honored her by dedicating themselves to the affairs of love, and so too with the other Muses, according to the activity that honors each. And to Calliope, the oldest among them, and Urania, the next after her, who preside over the heavens and all discourse, human and divine, and sing with the sweetest voice, they report those who honor their special kind of music by leading a philosophical life.[131]

There are many reasons, then, why we should talk and not waste our afternoon in sleep.

PH. By all means, let's talk.

SO. Well, then, we ought to examine the topic we proposed just now: When is a speech well written and delivered, and when is it not? 259E

PH. Plainly.

SO. Won't someone who is to speak well and nobly have to have in mind the truth about the subject he is going to discuss?

PH. What I have actually heard about this, Socrates, my friend, is that it is not necessary for the intending orator to learn what is really just, but only what will seem just to the crowd who will act as judges. Nor again what is really good or noble, but only what will seem so. For that is what persuasion proceeds from, not truth. 260A

SO. Anything that wise men say, Phaedrus, "is not lightly to be cast aside";[132] we must consider whether it might be right. And what you just said, in particular, must not be dismissed.

---

131. Although they were usually referred to collectively in this period, each of the Muses was assigned to one of the arts—Terpsichore to dance and Erato to lyric poetry. Urania (whose name means "heavenly") was associated with astronomy. Calliope (who came to be the Muse of epic poetry) was accorded the highest honor in Hesiod's *Theogony* (line 80, ff.) as the Muse responsible for the ability of the high officials he calls "kings" to render good judgments that are persuasive and bring conflicts to an end.

132. "Is not lightly to be cast aside": *Iliad* 2.361.

PH. You're right.

So. Let's look at it this way, then.

PH. How?

260B So. Suppose I were trying to convince you that you should fight your enemies on horseback, and neither one of us knew what a horse is, but I happened to know this much about you, that Phaedrus believes a horse is the tame animal with the longest ears—

PH. But that would be ridiculous, Socrates.

So. Not quite yet, actually. But if I were seriously trying to convince you, having composed a speech in praise of the donkey in which I called it a horse and claimed that having such an animal is of immense value both at home and in military service, that it is good for fighting and for carrying your
260C baggage and that it is useful for much else besides—

PH. Well, that would be totally ridiculous.

So. Well, which is better? To be ridiculous and a friend? Or clever and an enemy?

PH. The former.

So. And so, when a rhetorician who does not know good from bad addresses a city which knows no better and attempts to sway it, not praising a miserable donkey as if it were a horse,[133] but bad as if it were good, and, having studied what the people believe, persuades them to do something
260D bad instead of good—with that as its seed, what sort of crop do you think rhetoric can harvest?

PH. A crop of really poor quality.

So. But could it be, my friend, that we have mocked the art of speaking more rudely than it deserves? For it might perhaps

---

133. "Miserable donkey": literally, "the shadow of a donkey," meaning a matter of no importance. An ancient commentator on Aristophanes' *Wasps*, 191, explains the origin of the story. A man rented a donkey to transport some things from Megara to Athens. As it was July, and noon, and the heat was terrible, the man stopped the donkey and sat in its shadow to cool off. The owner of the donkey, who was also there, claimed that the animal had been leased only for transporting baggage and not for providing shade. The two men had a terrible fight and ended up in court over it.

reply, "What bizarre nonsense! Look, I am not forcing anyone to learn how to make speeches without knowing the truth; on the contrary, my advice, for what it is worth, is to take me up only after mastering the truth. But I do make this boast: even someone who knows the truth couldn't produce conviction on the basis of a systematic art without me."

PH. Well, is that a fair reply? 260E

SO. Yes, it is—if, that is, the arguments now advancing upon rhetoric testify that it is an art. For it seems to me as if I hear certain arguments approaching and protesting that that is a lie and that rhetoric is not an art but an artless practice.[134] As the Spartan said, there is no genuine art of speaking without a grasp of truth, and there never will be.[135]

PH. We need to hear these arguments, Socrates. Come, produce 261A them, and examine them: What is their point? How do they make it?

SO. Come to us, then, noble creatures; convince Phaedrus, him of the beautiful offspring,[136] that unless he pursues philosophy properly he will never be able to make a proper speech on any subject either. And let Phaedrus be the one to answer.

PH. Let them put their questions.

SO. Well, then, isn't the rhetorical art, taken as a whole, a way of directing the soul by means of speech, not only in the lawcourts and on other public occasions but also in private?[137]

---

134. "Not an art but an artless practice": *atechnos tribē*. On *technē* see note 62 on 245a. For a similar criticism of rhetoric as artless, see *Gorgias* 462b–c.

135. "As the Spartan said": Spartans were proverbially laconic, so this could mean simply, "to put it bluntly"; but the word used for "genuine" (*etumos*) is unusual in Plato and may come from the Dorian dialect of the Spartans. It is used at 243a (in Stesichorus' palinode), at 244a ("there is no truth to that story"), and nowhere else in Plato.

136. "Beautiful offspring": Phaedrus' offspring are speeches or philosophical discussions. Cf. 242a–b and *Symposium* 209b–e.

137. Very similar to the definition of rhetoric Plato has Gorgias give at *Gorgias* 452e, except that Gorgias (1) does not mention private occasions, and (2) speaks simply of persuasion instead of "directing the soul"

261B   Isn't it one and the same art whether its subject is great or small, and no more to be held in esteem—if it is followed correctly—when its questions are serious than when they are trivial? Or what have you heard about all this?

PH. Well, certainly not what *you* have! Artful speaking and writing is found mainly in the lawcourts; also perhaps in the Assembly.[138] That's all I've heard.

SO. Well, have you only heard of the rhetorical treatises of Nestor and Odysseus—those they wrote in their spare time in Troy? Haven't you also heard of the works of Palamedes?[139]

(*psychagōgia*). Cf. also Socrates' broad account of rhetoric as persuasion at *Gorgias* 453d–454a.

Psychagōgia, literally "soul-leading," means something like "bewitchment." It evokes images of conjuring up souls from the underworld (see the play on words in Aristophanes, *Birds*, 1555—"unwashed Socrates calls up [*psychagōgei*] souls from the lake"). In the *Laws* the verb form of *psychagōgia* is used for the claims of those sophists who should be condemned to life imprisonment, their bodies to be cast across the borders of the state unburied (909b). Isocrates, however, uses it for the power of poetry that is denied to orators (*Evagoras* 10). In the *Timaeus* it is used for the irrational effect on the mind of images and phantasms (71a, cf. Xenophon, *Memorabilia* 3.10.6, and *Minos* 321a with Aristotle *Poetics* 1450a33–34).

138. Public speaking was at the center of all Greek political life (see Homer, *Iliad* 2.118–277), but it was especially prominent in Athens. Athenians prided themselves on their democratic Assembly, which could be influenced by any citizen who could speak well, regardless of his social rank. Effective speakers who did not hold office were known as demagogues. Athenian courts consisted of large juries of ordinary people—too many to bribe, but also too many to persuade without expert techniques of speaking. For an accused person, the ability to speak could make the difference between life and death, a point which paid teachers of rhetoric used to their advantage (*Gorgias* 485e–486b).

139. Nestor and Odysseus are Homeric heroes known for their speaking ability (*Iliad* 1.249, 3.223). Palamedes, who does not figure in Homer, was proverbial for his cunning. He tricked Odysseus into joining the Greek expedition against Troy (see Introduction, pp. ix–x). According to a tradition different from that on which Plato relies below (274d–275b), Palamedes was the inventor of the alphabet.

Discussion of Rhetoric

Ph. No, by Zeus, I haven't even heard of Nestor's—unless by 261C
Nestor you mean Gorgias, and by Odysseus, Thrasymachus
or Theodorus.[140]

So. Perhaps. But let's leave these people aside. Answer this
question yourself: What do adversaries do in the lawcourts?
Don't they speak on opposite sides? What else can we call
what they do?

Ph. That's it, exactly.

So. About what is just and what is unjust?

Ph. Yes.

So. And won't whoever does this artfully make the same thing 261D
appear to the same people sometimes just and sometimes,
when he prefers, unjust?

Ph. Of course.

So. And when he addresses the Assembly, he will make the city
approve a policy at one time as a good one, and reject it—
the very same policy—as just the opposite at another.

Ph. Right.

So. Now, don't we know that the Eleatic Palamedes is such an
artful speaker that his listeners will perceive the same things
to be both similar and dissimilar, both one and many, both
at rest and also in motion?[141]

Ph. Most certainly.

So. We can therefore find the practice of speaking on opposite
sides not only in the lawcourts and in the Assembly. Rather, 261E

---

140. Gorgias of Leontini was the most famous teacher of rhetoric who visited Athens. Two model speeches have survived, one in praise of Helen, the other in defense of Palamedes (DK 11 and 11a). About Thrasymachus of Chalcedon (cf. 267c) we know little beyond what we can infer from his appearance in Book 1 of the *Republic*; a few paragraphs of his rhetoric survive (DK 1) and we may have a complete speech as well. The case can be made that a speech now attributed by most scholars to Critias should be assigned to Thrasymachus. From Theodorus of Byzantium (not to be confused with the mathematician who appears in the *Theaetetus*) we have no fragments (but see 266e and Aristotle *Rhetoric* 3.13.5).

141. The Eleatic Palamedes is Zeno of Elea, the author of the famous paradoxes about motion (see *Parmenides* 127d–128a).

it seems that one single art—if, of course, it is an art in the first place—governs all speaking. By means of it one can make out as similar anything that can be so assimilated, to everything to which it can be made similar, and expose anyone who tries to hide the fact that that is what he is doing.

PH. What do you mean by that?

SO. I think it will become clear if we look at it this way. Where is deception most likely to occur—regarding things that differ much or things that differ little from one another?

262A PH. Regarding those that differ little.

SO. At any rate, you are more likely to escape detection, as you shift from one thing to its opposite, if you proceed in small steps rather than in large ones.

PH. Without a doubt.

SO. Therefore, if you are to deceive someone else and to avoid deception yourself, you must know precisely the respects in which things are similar and dissimilar to one another.

PH. Yes, you must.

SO. And is it really possible for someone who doesn't know what each thing truly is to detect a similarity—whether large or small—between something he doesn't know and anything else?

262B PH. That is impossible.

SO. Clearly, therefore, the state of being deceived and holding beliefs contrary to what is the case comes upon people by reason of certain similarities.

PH. That is how it happens.

SO. Could someone, then, who doesn't know what each thing is ever have the art to lead others little by little through similarities away from what is the case on each occasion to its opposite? Or could he escape this being done to himself?

PH. Never.

262C SO. Therefore, my friend, the art of a speaker who doesn't know the truth and chases opinions instead is likely to be a ridiculous thing—not an art at all!

PH. So it seems.

So. So, shall we look for instances of what we called the artful and the artless in the speech of Lysias you carried here and in our own speeches?

PH. That's the best thing to do—because, as it is, we are talking quite abstractly, without enough examples.

So. In fact, by some chance the two speeches[142] do, as it seems, contain an example of the way in which someone who knows the truth can toy with his audience and mislead them. For my part, Phaedrus, I hold the local gods responsible for this—also, perhaps, the messengers of the Muses[143] who are singing over our heads may have inspired me with this gift: certainly I don't possess any art of speaking.

262D

PH. Fine, fine. But explain what you mean.

So. Come, then—read me the beginning of Lysias' speech.

PH. "You understand my situation: I've told you how good it would be for us, in my opinion, if we could work this out. In any case, I don't think I should lose the chance to get what I am asking for, merely because I don't happen to be in love with you. A man in love will wish he had not done you any favors—"[144]

262E

So. Stop. Our task is to say how he fails and writes artlessly. Right?

---

142. "The two speeches": Socrates' two speeches, since Socrates does not wish to imply that Lysias knows the truth about his subject, and since the messengers mentioned in the next sentence cannot have had an influence on Lysias in any case. See Rowe's note on 262c10–d6. In contrast to our approach, Hackforth, *Plato's "Phaedrus"*; Ferrari, *Listening to the Cicadas*; and de Vries hold that the two speeches are Lysias' speech and Socrates' two taken as one (as at 265c).

143. "Messengers of the Muses": *prophētai*, "interpreters" (see note 58). The messengers are the cicadas (259c).

144. In quoting the speech from 231e, here and at 263e Phaedrus changes the word order slightly, from *genomenōn toutōn* to *toutōn genomenōn*, from "if this could be *worked out*" to "if *this* could be worked out."

263A PH. Yes.

SO. Now isn't this much absolutely clear: We are in accord with one another about some of the things we discourse about and in discord about others?

PH. I think I understand what you are saying; but, please, can you make it a little clearer?

SO. When someone utters the word "iron" or "silver," don't we all think of the same thing?

PH. Certainly.

SO. But what happens when we say "just" or "good"? Doesn't each one of us go in a different direction? Don't we differ with one another and even with ourselves?

PH. We certainly do.

263B SO. Therefore, we agree about the former and disagree about the latter.

PH. Right.

SO. Now in which of these two cases are we more easily deceived? And when does rhetoric have greater power?

PH. Clearly, when we wander in different directions.

SO. It follows that whoever wants to acquire the art of rhetoric must first make a systematic division and grasp the particular character of each of these two kinds of thing, both the kind where most people wander in different directions and the kind where they do not.

263C PH. What a splendid thing, Socrates, he will have understood if he grasps *that!*

SO. Second, I think, he must not be mistaken about his subject; he must have a sharp eye for the class to which whatever he is about to discuss belongs.

PH. Of course.

SO. Well, now, what shall we say about love? Does it belong to the class where people differ or to that where they don't?

PH. Oh, surely the class where they differ. Otherwise, do you think you could have spoken of it as you did a few minutes ago, first saying that it is harmful both to lover and beloved and then immediately afterward that it is the greatest good?

Discussion of Rhetoric

So. Very well put. But now tell me this—I can't remember at all 263D because I was completely possessed by the gods: Did I define love at the beginning of my speech?

Ph. Oh, absolutely, by Zeus, you most certainly did.

So. Alas, how much more artful with speeches the Nymphs, daughters of Achelous, and Pan, son of Hermes, are, according to what you say, than Lysias, son of Cephalus! Or am I wrong? Did Lysias too, at the start of his love-speech, compel us to assume that love is the single thing that he 263E himself wanted it to be? Did he then complete his speech by arranging everything in relation to that? Will you read its opening once again?

Ph. If you like. But what you are looking for is not there.

So. Read it, so that I can hear it in his own words.

Ph. "You understand my situation: I've told you how good it would be for us, in my opinion, if we could work this out. In any case, I don't think I should lose the chance to get what I am asking for, merely because I don't happen to be 264A in love with you. A man in love will wish he had not done you any favors, once his desire dies down—"

So. He certainly seems a long way from doing what we wanted. He doesn't even start from the beginning but from the end, making his speech swim upstream on its back. His first words are what a lover would say to his boy as he was concluding his speech. Am I wrong, Phaedrus, dear heart?[145]

Ph. Well, Socrates, that was the end for which he gave the 264B speech!

So. And what about the rest? Don't the parts of the speech appear to have been thrown together at random? Is it evident that the second point had to be made second for some compelling reason?[146] Is that so for any of the parts? I at least—

---

145. "End": *teleutē* (see 253c). "Dear heart": literally "dear head," an epic formula (*Iliad* 8.281).

146. "For some compelling reason?" The Greek is *anankē* (necessity). Socrates' first speech made conspicuously pedantic use of *anankē* at each stage in the argument, deriving conclusions by logical necessity from his definition of love.

of course I know nothing about such matters—thought the author said just whatever came to mind next, though not without a certain noble willfulness. But you, do you know any principle of speech-composition compelling him to place these things one after another in this order?

264C PH. It's very generous of you to think that I can understand his reasons so clearly.

SO. But surely you will admit at least this much: Every speech must be put together like a living creature, with a body of its own; it must be neither without head nor without legs; and it must have a middle and extremities that are fitting both to one another and to the whole work.

PH. How could it be otherwise?

SO. But look at your friend's speech: Is it like that or is it otherwise? Actually, you'll find that it's just like the epigram people say is inscribed on the tomb of Midas the Phrygian.[147]

264D PH. What epigram is that? And what's the matter with it?

SO. It goes like this:

> A maid of bronze am I, on Midas' tomb I lie
> As long as water flows, and trees grow tall
> Shielding the grave where many come to cry
> That Midas rests here I say to one and all.

264E I'm sure you notice that it makes no difference at all which of its verses comes first, and which last.

PH. You are making fun of our speech, Socrates.

SO. Well, then, if that upsets you, let's leave that speech aside—even though I think it has plenty of very useful examples, provided one tries to emulate them as little as possible—and turn to the others. I think it is important for students of speechmaking to pay attention to one of their features.

---

147. The historical Midas was king of Phrygia in the eighth century B.C.

PH. What do you mean? 265A

SO. They were in a way opposite to one another. One claimed that one should give one's favors to the lover; the other, to the non-lover.

PH. Most manfully, too.

SO. I thought you were going to say "madly," which would have been the truth, and is also just what I was looking for: We did say, didn't we, that love is a kind of madness?

PH. Yes.

SO. And that there are two kinds of madness, one produced by human illness, the other by a divinely inspired release from normally accepted behavior?

PH. Certainly. 265B

SO. We also distinguished four parts within the divine kind and connected them to four gods. Having attributed the inspiration of the prophet to Apollo, of the mystic to Dionysus, of the poet to the Muses, and the fourth part of madness to Aphrodite and to Love, we said that the madness of love is the best. We used a certain sort of image to describe love's passion; perhaps it had a measure of truth in it, though it may also have led us astray. And having whipped up a not altogether implausible speech, we sang playfully, but also 265C appropriately and respectfully, a storylike hymn to my master and yours, Phaedrus—to Love, who watches over beautiful boys.

PH. And I listened to it with the greatest pleasure.

SO. Let's take up this point about it right away: How was the speech able to proceed from censure to praise?[148]

PH. What exactly do you mean by that?

SO. Well, everything else in it really does appear to me to have been spoken in play. But part of it was given with Fortune's guidance, and there were in it two kinds of things the nature 265D of which it would be quite wonderful to grasp by means of a systematic art.

---

148. Here Socrates treats his two speeches as one (see note 142).

PH. Which things?

SO. The first consists in seeing together things that are scattered about everywhere and collecting them into one kind, so that by defining each thing we can make clear the subject of any instruction we wish to give.[149] Just so with our discussion of love: Whether its definition was or was not correct, at least it allowed the speech to proceed clearly and consistently with itself.

PH. And what is the other thing you are talking about, Socrates?

265E SO. This, in turn, is to be able to cut up each kind according to its species along its natural joints, and to try not to splinter any part, as a bad butcher might do. In just this way, our two speeches placed all mental derangements into one common 266A kind. Then, just as each single body has parts that naturally come in pairs of the same name (one of them being called the right-hand and the other the left-hand one),[150] so the speeches, having considered unsoundness of mind to be by nature one single kind within us, proceeded to cut it up—the first speech cut its left-hand part, and continued to cut until it discovered among these parts a sort of love that can be called "left-handed," which it correctly denounced; the second speech, in turn, led us to the right-hand part of madness; discovered a love that shares its name with the 266B other but is actually divine; set it out before us, and praised it as the cause of our greatest goods.

PH. You are absolutely right.

SO. Well, Phaedrus, I am myself a lover of these divisions and collections, so that I may be able to think and to speak; and if I believe that someone else is capable of discerning a single thing that is also by nature capable of encompassing many,[151]

---

149. On collecting many things into one kind, see 249c. Here, by introducing the idea of instruction, Socrates enlarges the context of rhetoric to include teaching (see Rowe's note).

150. The point is that each body has two hands, two feet, etc. The members of each pair are called the same (e.g., "hands") and are differentiated according to whether they are on the right or the left side.

151. "By nature capable of encompassing many": This is the version in the manuscripts, which read *pephukos*. Many editors, unable to make

I follow "straight behind, in his tracks, as if he were a god."[152]
God knows whether this is the right name for those who can do this correctly or not, but so far I have always called them "dialecticians." But tell me what I must call them now that we have learned all this from Lysias and you. Or is it just that art of speaking that Thrasymachus and the rest of them use, which has made them masters of speechmaking and capable of producing others like them—anyhow those who are willing to bring them gifts and to treat them as if they were kings?

PH. They may behave like kings, but they certainly lack the knowledge you're talking about. No, it seems to me that you are right in calling the sort of thing you mentioned dialectic; but, it seems to me, rhetoric still eludes us.

So. What are you saying? Could there be anything valuable which is independent of the methods I mentioned and is still grasped by art? If there is, you and I must certainly honor it, and we must say what part of rhetoric it is that has been left out.

PH. Well, there's quite a lot, Socrates: everything, at any rate, written up in the books on the art of speaking.

So. You were quite right to remind me. First, I believe, there is the Preamble with which a speech must begin. This is what you mean, isn't it—the fine points of the art?

PH. Yes.

So. Second come the Statement of Facts and the Evidence of Witnesses concerning it; third, Indirect Evidence; fourth, Claims to Plausibility. And I believe at least that excellent Byzantine word-wizard adds Confirmation and Supplementary Confirmation.

---

sense of the manuscript reading, wrongly prefer *pephukota*, which would give either of two meanings: (1) It may modify both "one" and "many"—"a natural unity and a natural plurality" (most versions; Hackforth cites *Philebus* 17a and 18a in support); (2) it may modify the agent—"anyone else who has the natural capacity to look to one and many."

152. "Straight behind, in his track, as if he were a god": Plato has adapted this line from Homer, *Odyssey* 2.406.

PH. You mean the worthy Theodorus?[153]

267A SO. Quite. And he also adds Refutation and Supplementary Refutation, to be used both in prosecution and in defense. Nor must we forget the most excellent Evenus of Paros,[154] who was the first to discover Covert Implication and Indirect Praise and who—some say—has even arranged Indirect Censures in verse as an aid to memory: a wise man indeed! And Tisias[155] and Gorgias? How can we leave them out when it is they who realized that what is likely must be held in higher honor than what is true; they who, by the power of
267B their language, make small things appear great and great things small; they who express modern ideas in ancient garb, and ancient ones in modern dress; they who have discovered how to argue both concisely and at infinite length about any subject? Actually, when I told Prodicus[156] this last, he laughed and said that only he had discovered the art of proper speeches: What we need are speeches that are neither long nor short but of the right length.

PH. Brilliantly done, Prodicus!

SO. And what about Hippias?[157] How can we omit him? I am sure our friend from Elis would cast his vote with Prodicus.

---

153. See note 140.

154. Evenus of Paros was active as a sophist toward the end of the fifth century B.C. He is mentioned elsewhere in Plato (*Apology* 20b, *Phaedo* 60c–61c), but only a few tiny fragments of his work survive.

155. Tisias of Syracuse, with Corax, is credited with the founding of the Sicilian school of rhetoric, represented by Gorgias and Polus. For Gorgias, see note 140. Unlike sophists such as Hippias, Protagoras, and Prodicus, teachers of this school confined themselves to the art of speaking. For Corax's teaching on "what is likely" (*eikos*), see Aristotle *Rhetoric* 2.24.11.

156. Prodicus of Ceos, who lived from about 470 till after 400 B.C., is frequently mentioned by Plato in connection with his ability to make fine verbal distinctions (*Protagoras* 339e–341d, *Meno* 75e, *Euthydemus* 277e; cf. Aristotle, *Topics* 122b22). A parody of his style is to be found at *Protagoras* 337a–c, and a paraphrase of his speech on "The choice of Heracles" is in Xenophon, *Memorabilia* 2.1.21–33.

157. Hippias of Elis was born in the mid fifth century and traveled widely teaching a variety of subjects, including mathematics, astron-

Discussion of Rhetoric

PH. Certainly.

SO. And what shall we say of the whole gallery of terms Polus[158] set up—speaking with Reduplication, Speaking in Maxims, Speaking in Images—and of the terms Licymnius gave him as a present to help him explain Good Diction?[159] 267C

PH. But didn't Protagoras actually use similar terms?[160]

SO. Yes, Correct Diction, my boy, and other wonderful things. As to the art of making speeches bewailing the evils of poverty and old age, the prize, in my judgment, goes to the mighty Chalcedonian.[161] He it is also who knows best how to inflame a crowd and, once they are inflamed, how to hush them again with his words' magic spell, as he says himself. And let's not forget that he is as good at producing slander as he is at refuting it, whatever its source may be. 267D

As to the way of ending a speech, everyone seems to be in agreement, though some call it Recapitulation and others by some other name.

PH. You mean, summarizing everything at the end and reminding the audience of what they've heard?

---

omy, harmony, mnemonics, ethics, and history as well as public speaking. There is a parody of his style at *Protagoras* 337d–338b.

158. Polus was a pupil of Gorgias; Plato represents him in the *Gorgias*, esp. at 448c and 471a–c. He was said to have composed an *Art of Rhetoric* (*Gorgias*, 462b). "Gallery of terms": *mouseia logōn*. Hackforth interprets this as the title of another of his works (*The Muses' Treasury of Phrases*). This interpretation is rather unlikely: As Rowe remarks in his note on this passage, it destroys the syntax and gives an anachronistic meaning to *mouseiōn*.

159. Licymnius of Chios was a dithyrambic poet and teacher of rhetoric. See Aristotle, *Rhetoric* 3.13.5, 3.2.13.

160. Protagoras of Abdera, whose life spanned most of the fifth century B.C., was the most famous of the early sophists. Only a handful of short fragments of his work survive, but we have a vivid portrayal of him in Plato's *Protagoras* and an intriguing reconstruction of his epistemology in the *Theaetetus*. With his interest in Correct Diction (*orthoepeia*) compare *Cratylus* 391c (with 400d–401a) and *Protagoras* 338e–339d.

161. Literally, "the might of the Chalcedonian": a Homeric figure referring to Thrasymachus, who came from Chalcedon. See note 140.

So. That's what I mean. And if you have anything else to add about the art of speaking—

Ph. Only minor points, not worth making.

268A So. Well, let's leave minor points aside. Let's hold what we do have closer to the light so that we can see precisely the power of the art these things produce.

Ph. A very great power, Socrates, especially in front of a crowd.

So. Quite right. But now, my friend, look closely: Do you think, as I do, that its fabric is a little threadbare?

Ph. Can you show me?

So. All right, tell me this. Suppose someone came to your friend Eryximachus or his father Acumenus and said: "I know treat-
268B ments to raise or lower (whichever I prefer) the temperature of people's bodies; if I decide to, I can make them vomit or make their bowels move, and all sorts of things. On the basis of this knowledge, I claim to be a physician; and I claim to be able to make others physicians as well by imparting it to them." What do you think they would say when they heard that?

Ph. What could they say? They would ask him if he also knew to whom he should apply such treatments, when, and to what extent.

So. What if he replied, "I have no idea. My claim is that whoever
268C learns from me will manage to do what you ask on his own"?

Ph. I think they'd say the man's mad if he thinks he's a doctor just because he read a book or happened to come across a few potions; he knows nothing of the art.

So. And suppose someone approached Sophocles and Euripides and claimed to know how to compose the longest passages on trivial topics and the briefest ones on topics of great importance, that he could make them pitiful if he wanted,
268D or again, by contrast, terrifying and menacing, and so on. Suppose further that he believed that by teaching this he was imparting the knowledge of composing tragedies—

Ph. Oh, I am sure they too would laugh at anyone who thought a tragedy was anything other than the proper arrangement of these things: They have to fit with one another and with the whole work.

So. But I am sure they wouldn't reproach him rudely. They would react more like a musician confronted by a man who thought he had mastered harmony because he was able to produce the highest and lowest notes on his strings. The musician would not say fiercely, "You stupid man, you are out of your mind!" As befits his calling, he would speak more gently: "My friend, though that too is necessary for understanding harmony, someone who has gotten as far as you have may still know absolutely nothing about the subject. What you know is what it's necessary to learn before you study harmony, but not harmony itself." 268E

Ph. That's certainly right.

So. So Sophocles would also tell the man who was showing off to them that he knew the preliminaries of tragedy, but not the art of tragedy itself. And Acumenus would say his man knew the preliminaries of medicine, but not medicine itself. 269A

Ph. Absolutely.

So. And what if the "honey-tongued Adrastus" (or perhaps Pericles)[162] were to hear of all the marvelous techniques we just discussed—Speaking Concisely and Speaking in Images and all the rest we listed and proposed to examine under the light? Would he be angry or rude, as you and I were, with those who write of those techniques and teach them as if they are rhetoric itself, and say something coarse to them? Wouldn't he—being wiser than we are—reproach us as well and say, "Phaedrus and Socrates, you should not be angry with these people—you should be sorry for them. The reason 269B

---

162. "'The honey-tongued Adrastus' (or perhaps Pericles)": Socrates is pairing the Athenian statesman Pericles with the mythical Adrastus, just as he paired teachers of rhetoric with Homeric heroes at 261c.

Pericles, who dominated Athens from the 450s until his death in 429 B.C., was famous as the most successful orator-politician of his time. For an example of his oratory, see the funeral speech reconstructed by Thucydides at 2.35–46 with the historian's verdict at 2.65. Socrates takes a more critical view at *Gorgias* 503c and 515c–516d (but see *Meno* 94b).

The quotation is from the early Spartan poet Tyrtaeus, fragment 9.8. Adrastus is a legendary warrior hero of Argos, one of the main characters in Euripides' *Suppliants*.

they cannot define rhetoric is that they are ignorant of dialectic. It is their ignorance that makes them think they have discovered what rhetoric is when they have mastered only what it is necessary to learn as preliminaries. So they teach these preliminaries and imagine their pupils have received a full course in rhetoric, thinking the task of using each of them persuasively and putting them together into a whole speech is a minor matter, to be worked out by the pupils from their own resources"?

PH. Really, Socrates, the art these men present as rhetoric in their courses and handbooks is no more than what you say. In my judgment, at least, your point is well taken. But how, from what source, could one acquire the art of the true rhetorician, the really persuasive speaker?

So. Well, Phaedrus, becoming good enough to be an accomplished competitor is probably—perhaps necessarily—like everything else. If you have a natural ability for rhetoric, you will become a famous rhetorician, provided you supplement your ability with knowledge and practice. To the extent that you lack any one of them, to that extent you will be less than perfect. But, insofar as there is an art of rhetoric, I don't believe the right method for acquiring it is to be found in the direction Lysias and Thrasymachus have followed.

PH. Where can we find it then?

So. My dear friend, maybe we can see now why Pericles was in all likelihood the greatest rhetorician of all.

PH. How is that?

So. All the great arts require endless talk and ethereal speculation[163] about nature: This seems to be what gives them their lofty point of view and universal applicability. That's just what Pericles mastered—besides having natural ability. He

---

163. "Endless talk and ethereal speculation": These words (*adoleschia kai meteorologia*) represent the popular view of philosophy and the new learning (Aristophanes *Clouds* 1480 ff.). Since Plato took a dim view of Pericles' oratory (*Gorgias* 515), this paragraph is probably ironic. For Socrates' attitude toward Anaxagoras, see *Apology* 26d–e. For similar criticism of philosophy, see *Republic* 488e–489e and *Theaetetus* 175b ff.

Discussion of Rhetoric

came across Anaxagoras, who was just that sort of man, got his full dose of ethereal speculation, and understood the nature of mind and mindlessness[164]—just the subject on which Anaxagoras had the most to say. From this, I think, he drew for the art of rhetoric what was useful to it.

PH. What do you mean by that?

SO. Well, isn't the method of medicine in a way the same as the method of rhetoric? 270B

PH. How so?

SO. In both cases we need to determine the nature of something—of the body in medicine, of the soul in rhetoric. Otherwise, all we'll have will be an empirical and artless practice. We won't be able to supply, on the basis of an art, a body with the medicines and diet that will make it healthy and strong, or a soul with the reasons and customary rules for conduct that will impart to it the convictions and virtues we want.

PH. That is most likely, Socrates.

SO. Do you think, then, that it is possible to reach a serious understanding of the nature of the soul without understanding the nature of the world as a whole? 270C

PH. Well, if we're to listen to Hippocrates, Asclepius' descendant,[165] we won't even understand the body if we don't follow that method.

SO. He speaks well, my friend. Still, Hippocrates aside, we must consider whether argument supports that view.

PH. I agree.

SO. Consider, then, what both Hippocrates and true argument say about nature. Isn't this the way to think systematically about the nature of anything? First, we must consider 270D

---

164. "Mind and *mindlessness*": reading *anoias* with the manuscripts.

165. Hippocrates, who was contemporary with Socrates, was the famous doctor whose name is given to the Hippocratic Oath. None of the written works that have come down to us under his name express the view attributed to him in what follows. All doctors were said to be descendants of Asclepius, hero and god of healing.

whether the object regarding which we intend to become experts and capable of transmitting our expertise is simple or complex. Then, if it is simple, we must investigate its power: What things does it have what natural power of acting upon? By what things does it have what natural disposition to be acted upon? If, on the other hand, it takes many forms, we must enumerate them all and, as we did in the simple case, investigate how each is naturally able to act upon what and how it has a natural disposition to be acted upon by what.

PH. It seems so, Socrates.

270E SO. Proceeding by any other method would be like walking with the blind. Conversely, whoever studies anything on the basis of an art must never be compared to the blind or the deaf. On the contrary, it is clear that someone who teaches another to make speeches as an art will demonstrate precisely the essential nature of that to which speeches are to be applied. And that, surely, is the soul.

PH. Of course.

271A SO. This is therefore the object toward which the speaker's whole effort is directed, since it is in the soul that he attempts to produce conviction. Isn't that so?

PH. Yes.

SO. Clearly, therefore, Thrasymachus and anyone else who teaches the art of rhetoric seriously will, first, describe the soul with absolute precision and enable us to understand what it is: whether it is one and homogeneous by nature or takes many forms, like the shape of bodies, since, as we said, that's what it is to demonstrate the nature of something.

PH. Absolutely.

SO. Second, he will explain how, in virtue of its nature, it acts and is acted upon by certain things.

PH. Of course.

271B SO. Third, he will classify the kinds of speech and of soul there are, as well as the various ways in which they are affected, and explain what causes each. He will then coordinate each kind of soul with the kind of speech appropriate to it. And he will give instructions concerning the reasons why one

Discussion of Rhetoric

kind of soul is necessarily convinced by one kind of speech while another necessarily remains unconvinced.

PH. This, I think, would certainly be the best way.

So. In fact, my friend, no speech will ever be a product of art, whether it is a model[166] or one actually given, if it is delivered or written in any other way—on this or on any other subject. But those who now write *Arts of Rhetoric*—we were just discussing them[167]—are cunning people: they hide the fact that they know very well everything about the soul. Well, then, until they begin to speak and write in this way, we mustn't allow ourselves to be convinced that they write on the basis of the art.   271C

PH. What way is that?

So. It's very difficult to speak the actual words, but as to how one should write in order to be as artful as possible—that I am willing to tell you.

PH. Please do.

So. Since the nature of speech is in fact to direct the soul, whoever intends to be a rhetorician must know how many kinds of soul there are. Their number is so-and-so many; each is of such-and-such a sort; hence some people have such-and-such a character and others have such-and-such. Those distinctions established, there are, in turn, so-and-so many kinds of speech, each of such-and-such a sort. People of such-and-such a character are easy to persuade by speeches of such-and-such a sort in connection with such-and-such an issue for this particular reason, while people of such-and-such another sort are difficult to persuade for those particular reasons.   271D

The orator must learn all this well, then put his theory into practice and develop the ability to discern each kind   271E

---

166. In contrast to an actual speech given in an assembly or court of law, a model speech, or *epideixis*, was presented to display an orator's skill and to serve as an example for students. Gorgias has just given such a speech at *Gorgias* 447b–c. Lysias' speech above is also, of course, such a display.

167. See 266c ff.

272A clearly as it occurs in the actions of real life. Otherwise he won't be any better off than he was when he was still listening to those discussions in school. He will now not only be able to say what kind of person is convinced by what kind of speech; on meeting someone he will be able to discern what he is like and make clear to himself that the person actually standing in front of him is of just this particular sort of character he had learned about in school—to that he must now apply speeches of such-and-such a kind in this particular way in order to secure conviction about such-and-such an issue. When he has learned all this—when, in addition, he has grasped the right occasions[168] for speaking and for holding back; and when he has also understood when the time is right for Speaking Concisely or Appealing to Pity or Exaggeration or for any other of the kinds of speech he has learned and when it is not—then, and only then, will he have finally mastered the art well and completely. But if his

272B speaking, his teaching, or his writing lacks any one of these elements and he still claims to be speaking with art, you'll be better off if you don't believe him.

"Well, Socrates and Phaedrus," the author of this discourse might say, "do you agree? Could we accept an art of speaking presented in any other terms?"

PH. That would be impossible, Socrates. Still, it's evidently rather a major undertaking.

So. You're right. And that's why we must turn all our arguments every which way and try to find some easier and shorter

272C route to the art: we don't want to follow a long rough path for no good reason when we can choose a short smooth one instead.

---

168. "The right occasions": The concept of *kairos* or the right occasion to say this or that was at the center of ancient rhetorical theory. According to Dionysius of Halicarnassus, a critic of the first century B.C., *kairos* was "the best measure of what gives pleasure or the opposite" in a speech. He goes on to say that Gorgias was the first to write about it, but that no expert general account could be given (*On Literary Composition*, 12). On the appeal to *kairos* in matters of love, see Pindar's fragments in the Appendix.

Now, try to remember if you've heard anything helpful from Lysias or anybody else. Speak up.

PH. It's not for lack of trying, but nothing comes to mind right now.

SO. Well, then, shall I tell you something I've heard people say who care about this topic?

PH. Of course.

SO. We do claim, after all, Phaedrus, that it is fair to give the wolf's side of the story as well.

PH. That's just what you should do.

272D

SO. Well, these people say that there is no need to be so solemn about all this and stretch it out to such lengths. For the fact is, as we said ourselves at the beginning of this discussion,[169] that one who intends to be an able rhetorician has no need to know the truth about the things that are just or good or yet about the people who are such either by nature or upbringing. No one in a lawcourt, you see, cares at all about the truth of such matters. They only care about what is convincing. This is called "the likely," and that is what a man who intends to speak according to art should concentrate on. Sometimes, in fact, whether you are prosecuting or defending a case, you must not even say what actually happened, if it was not likely to have happened—you must say something that is likely instead. Whatever you say, you should pursue what is likely and leave the truth aside: the whole art consists in cleaving to that throughout your speech.[170]

272E

273A

PH. That's an excellent presentation of what people say who profess to be expert in speeches, Socrates. I recall that we

---

169. See 259e ff.

170. Most of the surviving evidence of early oratory shows that speakers appealed to what is likely or plausible (*eikos*) only when evidence such as eyewitness testimony was not available. The defense of Antiphon, however, appealed to *eikos* when the evidence was fairly clear against him. Although highly praised by Thucydides, the defense was unsuccessful (Antiphon 1 in Gagarin & Woodruff; Thucydides 8.68).

raised this issue briefly earlier on, but it seems to be their single most important point.

So. No doubt you've churned through Tisias' book quite carefully.[171] Then let Tisias tell us this also: By "the likely" does he mean anything but what is thought to be so by the crowd?

Ph. What else?

So. And it's likely it was when he discovered this clever and artful technique that Tisias wrote that if a weak but spunky man is taken to court because he beat up a strong but cowardly one and stole his cloak or something else, neither one should tell the truth.[172] The coward must say that the spunky man didn't beat him up all by himself, while the latter must rebut this by saying that only the two of them were there, and fall back on that well-worn plea, "How could a man like me attack a man like him?" The strong man, naturally, will not admit his cowardice, but will try to invent some other lie, and may thus give his opponent the chance to refute him. And in other cases, speaking as the art dictates will take similar forms. Isn't that so, Phaedrus?

Ph. Of course.

So. Phew! Tisias—or whoever else it was and whatever name he pleases to use for himself[173]—seems[174] to have discovered an art which he has disguised very well! But now, my friend, shall we or shall we not say to him—

---

171. "No doubt you've *churned through* Tisias' book quite carefully": For the colloquial verb in this sense, *patein* (literally, "thresh"), see Aristophanes, *Birds*, 471, and W. W. Merry's comment *ad loc*. For Tisias, see above 267a with note 155.

172. "Neither one should tell the truth": Antiphon uses a similar example as the hypothesis for his First Tetralogy, a set of four model speeches; in his example the man who is robbed is also killed, so there are no credible witnesses, and the only possible appeal is to *eikos*. Aristotle treats the use of likelihood in such a case in his *Rhetoric* 2.24.11; cf. 1.12.7.

173. Socrates may be referring to Corax, whose name happens also to be the Greek word for "crow." For Corax, see note 155 on 267a.

174. "Seems": *eoiken*. Literally, "is likely to."

Discussion of Rhetoric

PH. What? 273D

SO. This: "Tisias, some time ago, before you came into the picture, we were saying that people get the idea of what is likely through its similarity to the truth. And we just explained that in every case the person who knows the truth knows best how to determine similarities. So, if you have something new to say about the art of speaking, we shall listen. But if you don't, we shall remain convinced by the explanations we gave just before: No one will ever possess the art of speaking, to the extent that any human being can, unless 273E he acquires the ability to enumerate the sorts of characters to be found in any audience, to divide everything according to its kinds, and to grasp each single thing firmly by means of one form. And no one can acquire these abilities without great effort—a laborious effort a sensible man will make not in order to speak and act among human beings, but so as to be able to speak and act in a way that pleases the gods as much as possible. Wiser people than ourselves, Tisias, say that a reasonable man must put his mind to being pleasant not to his fellow slaves (though this may happen as a 274A side effect) but to his masters, who are wholly good.[175] So, if the way round is long, don't be astonished: we must make this detour for the sake of things that are very important, not for what you have in mind. Still, as our argument asserts, if that is what you want, you'll get it best as a result of pursuing our own goal."

PH. What you've said is wonderful, Socrates—if only it could be done!

SO. Yet surely whatever one must go through on the way to an 274B honorable goal is itself honorable.

PH. Certainly.

SO. Well, then, that's enough about artfulness and artlessness in connection with speaking.

---

175. This may refer to Antisthenes, who is supposed to have said, "If you want to live with the gods, learn philosophy; if among men, rhetoric" (Fragment 125 Mullack). Antisthenes was a student of Socrates who held that happiness comes from virtue, which in turn comes from understanding.

PH. Quite.

SO. What's left, then, is aptness and ineptness in connection with writing: What feature makes writing good, and what inept? Right?

PH. Yes.

SO. Well, do you know how best to please god when you either use words or discuss them in general?

PH. Not at all. Do you?

274C SO. I can tell you what I've heard the ancients said, though they alone know the truth. However, if we could discover that ourselves, would we still care about the speculations of other people?[176]

PH. That's a silly question. Still, tell me what you say you've heard.

SO. Well, this is what I've heard. Among the ancient gods of Naucratis[177] in Egypt there was one to whom the bird called the ibis is sacred. The name of that divinity was Theuth,[178]
274D and it was he who first discovered number and calculation,

---

176. The sense of the Greek is obscure. Socrates may be saying that only the ancients know whether the story he is about to relate is true. From here on, however, he focuses on the issue of truth in general and claims that if we could discover by ourselves what is true about aptness in writing we would not need to rely on stories told by other people. The argument that follows the story of Theuth, which he tells partly under pressure from Phaedrus, is his effort to establish the truth independently.

177. Naucratis was a Greek trading colony in Egypt. The story that follows is probably an invention of Plato's (see 275b3) in which he reworks elements from Egyptian and Greek mythology. It is appropriately set in Egypt, since the Egyptians were known in Greece for their ancient records and their efforts to retain the memory of the past (Herodotus 2.77). The story picks up the theme of the conflict between Zeus and Prometheus; see Rowe's note on the passage.

178. Theuth (or Thoth) is the Egyptian god of writing, measuring, and calculation, who is represented on early monuments by an ibis. The Greeks identified Thoth with Hermes, perhaps because of his role in weighing the soul. Thoth figures in a related story about the alphabet at *Philebus* 18b.

geometry and astronomy, as well as the games of draughts and dice, and, above all else, writing.

Now the king of all Egypt at that time was Thamus,[179] who lived in the great city in the upper region that the Greeks call Egyptian Thebes; Thamus they call Ammon.[180] Theuth came to exhibit his arts to him and urged him to disseminate them to all the Egyptians. Thamus asked him about the usefulness of each art, and while Theuth was explaining it, Thamus praised him for whatever he thought was right in his explanations and criticized him for whatever he thought was wrong.

274E

The story goes that Thamus said much to Theuth, both for and against each art, which it would take too long to repeat. But when they came to writing, Theuth said: "O King, here is something that, once learned, will make the Egyptians wiser and will improve their memory; I have discovered a potion for memory and for wisdom."[181] Thamus, however, replied: "O most expert Theuth, one man can give birth to the elements of an art, but only another can judge how they can benefit or harm those who will use them. And now, since you are the father of writing, your affection for it has made you describe its effects as the opposite of what they really are. In fact, it will introduce forgetfulness into the soul of those who learn it: they will not practice using their memory because they will put their trust in writing, which is external and depends on signs that belong to others, instead of trying to remember from the inside, completely on their own. You have not discovered a potion for remembering, but for reminding; you provide your students with

275A

---

179. Thamus is a Greek name for the god Ammon. As king of the Egyptian gods, Ammon was identified by Egyptians with the sun god Ra and by the Greeks with Zeus.
180. "Thamus they call Ammon": accepting Postgate's emendation of *Thamus* for *theon*. This implies that in Socrates' account Thamus is a god as well as the king.
181. "A *potion* for memory and for wisdom": *Pharmakon* ("potion") can refer to a medicinal drug, a poison, or a magical potion. Cf. its uses at 230d6 and 275a5.

the appearance of wisdom, not with its reality. Your invention will enable them to hear many things without being properly taught, and they will imagine that they have come to know much while for the most part they will know nothing. And they will be difficult to get along with, since they will merely appear to be wise instead of really being so."

PH. Socrates, you're very good at making up stories from Egypt or wherever else you want!

So. But, my friend, the priests of the temple of Zeus at Dodona say that the first prophecies were the words of an oak.[182] Everyone who lived at that time, not being as wise as you young ones are today, found it rewarding enough in their simplicity to listen to an oak or even a stone, so long as it was telling the truth, while it seems to make a difference to you, Phaedrus, who is speaking and where he comes from. Why, though, don't you just consider whether what he says is right or wrong?

PH. I deserved that, Socrates. And I agree that the Theban king was correct about writing.

So. Well, then, those who think they can leave written instructions for an art, as well as those who accept them, thinking that writing can yield results that are clear or certain, must be quite naive and truly ignorant of Ammon's prophetic judgment: otherwise, how could they possibly think that words that have been written down can do more than remind those who already know what the writing is about?

PH. Quite right.

So. You know, Phaedrus, writing shares a strange feature with painting. The offsprings of painting stand there as if they are alive, but if anyone asks them anything, they remain most solemnly silent. The same is true of written words. You'd think they were speaking as if they had some understanding, but if you question anything that has been said

---

182. "The first prophecies were the words of an oak": The oracle of Zeus was at Dodona in northwestern Greece. Homer reports the tradition that the message came from an oak (*Odyssey* 327–28). Herodotus tells a slightly different tale (2.55).

because you want to learn more, it continues to signify just that very same thing forever. When it has once been written down, every discourse roams about everywhere, reaching indiscriminately those with understanding no less than those who have no business with it, and it doesn't know to whom it should speak and to whom it should not. And when it is faulted and attacked unfairly, it always needs its father's support; alone, it can neither defend itself nor come to its own support.[183]

PH. You are absolutely right about that, too.

SO. Now tell me, can we discern another kind of discourse, a legitimate brother of this one? Can we say how it comes about, and how it is by nature better and more capable?

PH. Which one is that? How do you think it comes about?

SO. It is a discourse that is written down, with knowledge, in the soul of the listener; it can defend itself, and it knows for whom it should speak and for whom it should remain silent.

PH. You mean the living, breathing discourse of the man who knows, of which the written one can be fairly called an image.

SO. Absolutely right. And tell me this. Would a sensible farmer, who cared about his seeds and wanted them to yield fruit, plant them in all seriousness in the gardens of Adonis in the middle of the summer and enjoy watching them bear fruit within seven days? Or would he do this as an amusement and in honor of the holiday, if he did it at all?[184] Wouldn't he use his knowledge of farming to plant the seeds

---

183. Cf. *Protagoras* 347c–348a, where Socrates argues that poetry cannot explain itself in the absence of its author, though he does not explicitly connect this with writing. For a related complaint against writing see the *Seventh Letter* 344c. See also the essay "On Those Who Write Speeches" by Alcidamas, a pupil of Gorgias who was roughly contemporary with Plato.

184. Gardens of Adonis were pots or window boxes used for forcing plants during the festival of Adonis. It does seem difficult to believe, however, that seeds actually produced fruit within a week.

he cared for when it was appropriate and be content if they bore fruit seven months later?

276C PH. That's how he would handle those he was serious about, Socrates, quite differently from the others, as you say.

SO. Now what about the man who knows what is just, noble, and good? Shall we say that he is less sensible with his seeds than the farmer is with his?

PH. Certainly not.

SO. Therefore, he won't be serious about writing them in ink, sowing them, through a pen, with words that are as incapable of speaking in their own defense as they are of teaching the truth adequately.

PH. That wouldn't be likely.

276D SO. Certainly not. When he writes, it's likely he will sow gardens of letters for the sake of amusing himself, storing up reminders for himself "when he reaches forgetful old age"[185] and for everyone who wants to follow in his footsteps, and will enjoy seeing them sweetly blooming. And when others turn to different amusements, watering themselves with drinking parties and everything else that goes along with them, he will rather spend his time amusing himself with the things I have just described.

276E PH. Socrates, you are contrasting a vulgar amusement with the very noblest—with the amusement of a man who can while away his time telling stories of justice and the other matters you mentioned.[186]

SO. That's just how it is, Phaedrus. But it is much nobler to be serious about these matters, and use the art of dialectic. The dialectician chooses a proper soul and plants and sows within it discourse accompanied by knowledge—discourse capable of helping itself as well as the man who planted it,
277A which is not barren but produces a seed from which more

---

185. The diction here is poetic, but the source of this phrase, if one exists, is unknown.
186. Possibly a reference to the *Republic*, in which Socrates spends a great deal of time spinning a tale about justice.

Conclusion

discourse grows in the character of others. Such discourse makes the seed forever immortal and renders the man who has it as happy as any human being can be.

PH. What you describe is really much nobler still.

So. And now that we have agreed about this, Phaedrus, we are finally able to decide the issue.

PH. What issue is that?

So. The issue which brought us to this point in the first place: We wanted to examine the attack made on Lysias on account of his writing speeches, and to ask which speeches are written artfully and which not. Now, I think that we have answered that question clearly enough. 277B

PH. So it seemed; but remind me again how we did it.

So. First, you must know the truth concerning everything you are speaking or writing about; you must learn how to define each thing in itself; and, having defined it, you must know how to divide it into kinds until you reach something indivisible. Second, you must understand the nature of the soul, along the same lines; you must determine which kind of speech is appropriate to each kind of soul, prepare and arrange your speech accordingly, and offer a complex and elaborate speech to a complex soul and a simple speech to a simple one. Then, and only then, will you be able to use speech artfully, to the extent that its nature allows it to be used that way, either in order to teach or in order to persuade. This is the whole point of the argument we have been making. 277C

PH. Absolutely. That is exactly how it seemed to us.

So. Now how about whether it's noble or shameful to give or write a speech—when it could be fairly said to be grounds for reproach, and when not? Didn't what we said just a little while ago make it clear— 277D

PH. What was that?

So. That if Lysias or anybody else ever did or ever does write—privately or for the public, in the course of proposing some law—a political document which he believes to embody clear knowledge of lasting importance, then this writer deserves reproach, whether anyone says so or not. For to be unaware

277E of the difference between a dream-image and the reality of what is just and unjust, good and bad, must truly be grounds for reproach even if the crowd praises it with one voice.

PH. It certainly must be.

So. On the other hand, take a man who thinks that a written discourse on any subject can only be a great amusement, that no discourse worth serious attention has ever been written in verse or prose, and that those that are recited in public without questioning and explanation, in the manner of the 278A rhapsodes, are given only in order to produce conviction.[187] He believes that at their very best these can only serve as reminders to those who already know. And he also thinks that only what is said for the sake of understanding and learning, what is truly written in the soul concerning what is just, noble, and good can be clear, perfect, and worth serious attention: Such discourses should be called his own legitimate children, first the discourse he may have discovered already within himself and then its sons and brothers 278B who may have grown naturally in other souls insofar as these are worthy; to the rest, he turns his back. Such a man, Phaedrus, would be just what you and I both would pray to become.

PH. I wish and pray for things to be just as you say.

So. Well, then: our playful amusement regarding discourse is complete. Now you go and tell Lysias that we came to the spring which is sacred to the Nymphs and heard words 278C charging us to deliver a message to Lysias and anyone else who composes speeches, as well as to Homer and anyone else who has composed poetry either spoken or sung, and third, to Solon and anyone else who writes political documents that he calls laws: If any one of you has composed

---

187. "Those that are recited in public without questioning and explanation, in the manner of the rhapsodes, are given only to produce conviction": Rhapsodes were professional reciters of Homeric poetry; see the *Ion* for Socrates' demonstration that a famous rhapsode can move his audience to tears without being able to explain his material. For a similar charge against orators, see *Protagoras* 328e–329a.

Conclusion

these things with a knowledge of the truth, if you can defend your writing when you are challenged, and if you can yourself make the argument that your writing is of little worth, then you must be called by a name derived not from these writings but rather from those things that you are seriously pursuing. *278D*

PH. What name, then, would you give such a man?

So. To call him wise, Phaedrus, seems to me too much, and proper only for a god. To call him wisdom's lover—a philosopher—or something similar would fit him better and be more seemly.

PH. That would be quite appropriate.

So. On the other hand, if a man has nothing more valuable than what he has composed or written, spending long hours twisting it around, pasting parts together and taking them apart—wouldn't you be right to call him a poet or a speech writer or an author of laws? *278E*

PH. Of course.

So. Tell that, then, to your friend.

PH. And what about you? What shall you do? We must surely not forget your own friend.

So. Whom do you mean?

PH. The beautiful Isocrates.[188] What are you going to tell him, Socrates? What shall we say he is?

So. Isocrates is still young, Phaedrus. But I want to tell you what I foresee for him. *279A*

PH. What is that?

So. It seems to me that by his nature he can outdo anything that Lysias has accomplished in his speeches; and he also has a

---

188. Isocrates (436–338 B.C.) was an Athenian teacher and orator whose school was more famous in its day than Plato's Academy. The praise of Isocrates that follows may be genuine, but most scholars take it to be ironic. Isocrates made no secret of his contempt for the sort of abstract philosophy pursued by Plato, and Plato may have intended Isocrates to be the butt of his criticism of rhetoric in the *Phaedrus*. For a thorough discussion, see de Vries, pp. 15–18.

nobler character. So I wouldn't be at all surprised if, as he gets older and continues writing speeches of the sort he is composing now, he makes everyone who has ever attempted to compose a speech seem like a child in comparison. Even more so if such work no longer satisfies him and a higher, divine impulse leads him to more important things. For nature, my friend, has placed the love of wisdom in his mind.

That is the message I will carry to my beloved, Isocrates, from the gods of this place; and you have your own message for your Lysias.

PH. So it shall be. But let's be off, since the heat has died down a bit.

So. Shouldn't we offer a prayer to the gods here before we leave?

PH. Of course.

So. O dear Pan and all the other gods of this place, grant that I may be beautiful inside. Let all my external possessions be in friendly harmony with what is within. May I consider the wise man rich. As for gold, let me have as much as a moderate man could bear and carry with him.

Do we need anything else, Phaedrus? I believe my prayer is enough for me.

PH. Make it a prayer for me as well. Friends have everything in common.

So. Let's be off.

APPENDIX: EARLY GREEK LOVE POETRY

PLATO'S IMAGES FOR LOVE in the *Phaedrus* are frequently borrowed from poets, of whom he cites Sappho and Anacreon in particular. Here we offer verse translations of ancient bits of poetry that are closely related in theme or image to the speeches of the *Phaedrus*.

None of the poems is complete. The love poetry of early Greece survives mainly in the form of fragments that either were quoted by later Greek authors or came down to us on scraps of papyrus. Fragments are numbered as in the Loeb editions.[1]

SAPPHO lived on the island of Lesbos around the beginning of the sixth century B.C. She is reported to have said that Persuasion (*Peithô*) was the daughter of Aphrodite (Fr 90.1a, 200). Composed for a young woman at a feast, the first poem powerfully expresses the effects of passion on a lover's body.

---

1. D. A. Campbell, *Greek Lyric*, Volumes I–III (Cambridge, Mass., 1982–91). For the fragment from Pindar, see Gordon Kirkwood, *Selections from Pindar, Edited with an Introduction and Commentary* (American Philological Association, 1982).

Sappho, Fragment 31

> How like a god I feel he is,
> this man, when he sits close
> facing you, hearing
> > your sweet voice
>
> and seductive laughter—it jolts
> my heart into a flutter in my breast.
> One look at you, voice
> > gives out completely
>
> tongue turns to splinters, a gentle
> burst of flame runs under the skin,
> eyes don't see a thing, ears
> > whir and rumble,
>
> sweat pours down me, I shake
> all over, I go pale as green
> grass. I'm that close to being dead—
> > or so I feel to myself.
>
> But all this I must endure, because . . . .

Sappho, Fragment 42

> When the heart of a pigeon has gone cold
> She lets her wings droop . . .

Sappho, Fragment 130

> Love again! Limb-loosener,[2] he makes me shake,
> the bitter-sweet, the impossible creeping thing!

---

2. Cf. Hesiod, *Theogony* 120–122:

> And Love, who is most beautiful of gods immortal,
> the limb-loosener who enslaves the minds of men
> and gods, who overrides the plans they choose.

APPENDIX

Sappho, Fragment 47

> Love gave my mind
> a shake, like wind striking oaks on a mountain.

Sappho, Fragment 48

> You came to me; I longed for you;
> You cooled my mind when it flamed with desire.

IBYCUS is shrouded in mystery. He lived in the sixth century, spent time on the island of Samos, and wrote on a variety of subjects. He was most famous for his passionate love poetry. Cicero says he "burned with love more than the other poets," and the Palatine Anthology addresses him thus:

> . . . And you, Ibycus,
> who picked the sweet blooms of Persuasion and boys.[3]

Ibycus, Fragment 287[4]

> It's Love again! He lids his melting eyes
> with those dark waves
> and shoots out every beckoning charm
> to bowl me into the endless swarms
> of Aphrodite's snares.
>
> How I tremble when he comes on—
> I'm like a horse who has won his crown
> and now is old,
> but is forced once more beneath swift chariot yokes
> and comes to the races.

---

3. Testimonia 12 and 13 in Campbell.
4. Mentioned by Plato, *Parmenides* 137a.

Ibycus, Fragment 286

>Oh, I know how it is in the spring
>   when Japonica's in bloom
>and rivers of many waters bring
>   life to the unplucked fruit.
>Then the vineyards of the Maidens flower
>   on every shaded vine;
>all flourish in that restful hour—
>   but, oh, this can't be mine!
>All seasons are the same to Love,
>   it's always time to storm;
>thunder is always flashing over
>   my head, and there's a swarm
>of desiccating furies in my mind.
>   Love chews away my heart
>   from the roots, in the dark.

ANACREON (ca. 570–ca. 485 B.C.) was famous for his playful poems on wine and love. He was born in Asia Minor, lived in Thrace and on the island of Samos, and spent his later years in Athens, to which he was invited by the poetry-loving Hipparchus, whose brother was tyrant from 527 to 510. Anacreon speaks of "melting love,"[5] but he seems to have kept his distance from the sort of passion expressed in Sappho.

Anacreon, Fragment 402C

>Boys would love me for my words,
>since what I sing is delightful,
>I know how to say what is delightful.

Anacreon, Fragment 428

>Oh, I'm in love again and not in love,
>I've gone mad and I'm not mad.

---

5. Fragment 459.

APPENDIX

Anacreon, Fragment 359

> With Cleobulus I am in love,
> For Cleobulus I have gone mad,
> On Cleobulus I fix my eyes . . . .

Anacreon, Fragment 360

> Your face, boy, like a girl's—
> I follow you, you've no idea,
> you'll never know my soul's the team
> and you the chariot-driver.

Anacreon, Fragment 378

> I fly up to Olympus on light wings
> on account of Love, because a boy
> wishes not to enjoy his youth with me.[6]

Anacreon, Fragment 398

> The dice love plays
> are madness and confusion.

Anacreon, Fragment 396

> Bring water, bring wine, boy, and bring us flowers
> in garlands. Do it now, so that I may box against Love.

Anacreon, Fragment 346.2

> My boxing match was tough,
> but now I look up and raise my head.
> I owe you many thanks for my escape from Love,
> Dionysus, for my total release
> from the harsh bonds of Aphrodite. . . .
> Let wine be brought in a bowl,
> let water be brought bubbling . . .
> and delight . . . .

---

6. Why does the poet fly to Olympus? Probably to seek help from Aphrodite.

PINDAR, who was born in 518 B.C. and lived well into the fifth century, is known mainly for his poems in honor of the winners of contests such as those at Olympia. Legend has it that Pindar fell in love with Theoxenus late in his life, and died in his arms at the age of eighty.

Pindar, Fragment 123

>You should have cut love's harvest at the right time,
>>my heart, when we were young.
>But now these sunbeams flashing from Theoxenus' eyes—
>>anyone who catches sight of those
>and isn't tossed by waves of desire must have been
>>hammered out of steel or iron
>in his black heart
>
>at a cold flame, a man who has no honor from
>>Aphrodite of the darting eyes.
>Either he grinds away fiercely after money,
>>or else a woman's impudence
>has carried him off, down an entirely cold road,
>>in her service.[7] Me? Because of Her[8] I have been bitten,
>and in that sunlight
>
>I melt like the wax of sacred bees
>>every time I watch the fresh-limbed
>beauty of a boy. For surely in Tenedos,
>>Persuasion is at home, and Delight
>graces the boy, the son of Hagesilas . . . .

Pindar, Fragment 127

>>Yes, love may come, and, yes, love's
>>pleasure may be served—at the right time,
>>>when you, my heart, do not,
>>>beyond measured value, chase after the deed.

---

7. The meaning of this clause is uncertain.
8. "Her": Aphrodite.

SELECTED BIBLIOGRAPHY

Barnes, Jonathan. *The Presocratic Philosophers*. London and Boston: Routledge and Kegan Paul, 1979.
Brisson, Luc. *Platon: "Phèdre."* Paris: Flammarion, 1989.
Burger, Ronna. *Plato's "Phaedrus": A Defense of a Philosophic Art of Writing*. Birmingham: University of Alabama Press, 1980.
Burnet, John. *Platonis Opera*, vol. II. Oxford Classical Texts. Oxford: Clarendon Press, 1903.
Cole, Thomas. *The Origins of Rhetoric in Ancient Greece*. Baltimore and London: Johns Hopkins University Press, 1991.
Cooper, John M. "Plato, Isocrates and Cicero on the Independence of Oratory from Philosophy." Cleary, J. *Proceedings of the Boston Area Ancient Philosophy Colloquium* 1 (1985): 77–96.
Derrida, Jacques. "Plato's Pharmacy." *Dissemination*. Chicago: University of Chicago Press, 1981: 61–171.
de Vries, G. J. *A Commentary on the "Phaedrus" of Plato*. Amsterdam: Hackert, 1969.
Dover, K. J. *Greek Homosexuality*. Cambridge, Mass.: Harvard University Press, 1978.
———. *Lysias and the Corpus Lysiacum*. Berkeley and Los Angeles: University of California Press, 1968.
Diels, Hermann, and Kranz, Walther. *Die Fragmente der Vorsokratiker*, 6th ed. Dublin and Zürich, 1951.
Ferrari, G. R. F. *Listening to the Cicadas: A Study of Plato's "Phaedrus."* Cambridge Classical Studies. Cambridge: Cambridge University Press, 1987.
———. "Platonic Love." Kraut, Richard. *The Cambridge Companion to Plato*. Cambridge: Cambridge University Press, 1992: 248–276.
Foucault, Michel. *The Uses of Pleasure*. New York: Random House, 1985.
Gagarin, Michael, and Woodruff, Paul. *Early Greek Political Theory from Homer to the Sophists*. Cambridge: Cambridge University Press, 1995.
Gould, Thomas. *Platonic Love*. London: Routledge and Kegan Paul, 1963.
Griswold, Charles L. *Self-Knowledge in Plato's "Phaedrus."* New Haven: Yale University Press, 1986.
Hackforth, R. *Plato's "Phaedrus."* Cambridge: Cambridge University Press, 1932.

Heath, Malcolm. "The Unity of Plato's *Phaedrus*." *Oxford Studies in Ancient Philosophy* 7 (1987): 150–173.

———. "The Unity of the *Phaedrus*." *Oxford Studies in Ancient Philosophy* 7 (1987): 189–191.

Helmbold, W. C., and Holther, W. B. "The Unity of the *Phaedrus*." *University of California Publications in Classical Philology* 14 (1952): 387–417.

Kennedy, George. *The Art of Persuasion in Greece*. Princeton: Princeton University Press, 1963.

Kosman, L. A. "Platonic Love." Werkmeister, W. *Facets of Plato's Philosophy*. *Phronesis* Supplementary Volume II. Assen: Van Gorcum (1976): 53–69.

Mackenzie, Mary Margaret. "Paradox in Plato's *Phaedrus*." *Proceedings of the Cambridge Philological Society* N.S. 28 (1982): 64–76.

Moore, John D. "The Relation Between Plato's *Symposium* and *Phaedrus*."

Moravcsik, J. M. E. *Patterns in Plato's Thought*. Dordrecht and Boston: Reidel, 1973: 52–71.

Moravcsik, Julius, and Temko, Philip. *Plato on Beauty, Wisdom and the Arts*. Totowa, NJ: Rowman and Littlefield, 1982.

Nussbaum, Martha Craven. *The Fragility of Goodness: Luck and Ethics in Greek Tragedy and Philosophy*. Cambridge: Cambridge University Press, 1986.

Rowe, C. J. "The Argument and Structure of Plato's *Phaedrus*." *Proceedings of the Cambridge Philological Society* 32: 1986: 106–125.

———. "The Unity of the *Phaedrus*: A Reply to Heath." *Oxford Studies in Ancient Philosophy* 7 (1987): 175–188.

———. *Plato: Phaedrus, with Translation and Commentary*. Warminster: Aris and Phillips, 1986.

Schleiermacher, Friedrich. *Introductions to the Dialogues of Plato*. New York: Arno Press, 1973.

Thompson, W. H. *The Phaedrus of Plato, with English Notes and Dissertations*. London: Wittaker & Co., 1868.

White, David A. *Rhetoric and Reality in Plato's "Phaedrus."* Albany: State University of New York Press, 1993.